Baseball Memorabilia

A Babe Ruth single signature Wilson baseball in mint condition, large, bold and dark signature, commanded a winning bid of $6,600 at Guernsey's New York April 28–29 "The Sporting Auction." Because Ruth autographs are so highly priced, collectors must be wary of forged signatures.

BASEBALL MEMORABILIA

1834
1939
3 CENTS
CENTENNIAL OF BASEBALL
UNITED STATES POSTAGE

Robert Obojski

Sterling Publishing Co., Inc.   New York

These so-called "Strip Cards," made in about 1920 by a variety of manufacturers, portray a great many prominent players of that era, including Fred "Bonehead" Merkle, Dave "Beauty" Bancroft and Christy "Big Six" Mathewson ... but they aren't overly valuable since their backs are blank. Collectors much prefer cards that have stats and text on the back.

Library of Congress Cataloging-in-Publication Data

Obojski, Robert.
    Baseball memorabilia / Robert Obojski.
       p.   cm.
    Includes index.
    ISBN 0-8069-7290-4
    1. Baseball—Collectibles.   I. Title.
  GV875.2.O24 1991   90-23603
  796.357'075—dc20   CIP

10 9 8 7 6 5 4 3 2 1

© 1991 by Robert Obojski
Published by Sterling Publishing Company, Inc.
387 Park Avenue South, New York, N.Y. 10016
Distributed in Canada by Sterling Publishing
% Canadian Manda Group, P.O. Box 920, Station U
Toronto, Ontario, Canada M8Z 5P9
Distributed in Great Britain and Europe by Cassell PLC
Villiers House, 41/47 Strand, London WC2N 5JE, England
Distributed in Australia by Capricorn Ltd.
P.O. Box 665, Lane Cove, NSW 2066
Manufactured in the United States of America
All rights reserved

Sterling ISBN 0-8069-7290-4

Contents

Color section follows page 96

Introduction

Whether you are into baseball collectibles for profit, for nostalgia, or just for the fun of having memorabilia of the game surrounding your living quarters, you need to know what's in this book. If you go about collecting without knowing the total picture, you are bound to be less successful than those who are thoroughly acquainted with the suggestions and ideas in Bob Obojski's guidebook.

The fad turned into a mania in just a few years. Values soared. Kid stuff became big-time business. Baseball cards dominated the hobby, but they were not the end-all, nor were autographs the outer limit of the sport.

Caps, balls, gloves—pennants, programs, ticket stubs—shirts, uniforms, shoes—lockers, uprooted seats from the ball parks, even World Series rings—all came on the market and were paid for with big dollars as old-time players were enticed to sell everything they had. The mania began before historians like Obojski could publish books of guidance.

As the author points out, it's not too late to begin collecting, but you better hurry, and you better know what is wise and what may be unwise to buy or sell in this turbulent baseball memorabilia market.

Dedication

This book is dedicated to the late Arnold E. "Scotty" Maxwell, who for many years served as Superintendent of Grounds at both League Park and Municipal Stadium for the Cleveland Indians. (Cleveland for years was the only major league team that had two home parks).

During the late stages of World War II, the Indians found it almost impossible to hire grown men for the various "support jobs" like groundskeepers, ushers, scoreboard operators, et al, so they hired school kids like me, and many of us got our baptismal as wage earners under Scotty, who ruled the roost with a firm but fair hand, and who was not averse to giving one of his kids a pat on the behind for a job well done.

Scotty began working for the Indians as a young man in 1914, continued his association with the team well into the 1950s, and often reminisced about Cleveland's stars of the past like Nap Lajoie, Tris Speaker, Stan Coveleski, Steve O'Neill and Joe Wood. The air was always thick with talk about every aspect of baseball.

Scotty gave me all sorts of things to do at League Park: ushering in both the reserved sections and in the box seats (never an easy job when the place was jammed), sitting by the screen in back of home plate during games and retrieving foul balls to be returned to the umpire for re-use, holding one end of a 100-foot rope with a co-worker, who held the other end, along the third base line to prevent fans from walking on the infield after a game—and finally operating the electric scoreboard at Cleveland Municipal Stadium. We had to make sure we flashed the right count on the batter after every pitch because if we didn't the umpire would stop the game until we did.

During the nine years I worked for Scotty, I had the chance to see many baseball greats of the past come in and out of both parks. e.g., Bill Bradley, turn-of-the-century third baseman and a longtime Indians scout, who liked to play gin rummy with his cronies under the stands at League Park; Connie Mack, who managed the Philadelphia Athletics until he was 88 and who was always gracious with park workers; the legendary pitcher, Cy Young, who often came up to Cleveland from his Newcomerstown, Ohio, farm for Old-Timers events; and Jack Graney, outfielder on the Cleveland World Champions of 1920, who went on to broadcast Indians games on radio and TV for more than 20 years, and who could tell a baseball story better than anyone before or since.

Working for Scotty Maxwell and the Indians helped to form the foundation of my baseball education and made my boyhood and early adulthood very pleasant.

(Nikkon Sports, Tokyo)

Bob Obojski sits between immortals Shigeo Nagashima (#3) and Sadaharu Oh (#1) before a Tokyo Giants game with the Hiroshima Carp.

About the Author

Robert Obojski as a youth was an inveterate sandlot baseball player and worked his way through college by handling a number of part-time jobs with the Cleveland Indians—as a member of the grounds crew first, then operator of the electric scoreboard, and eventually as statistician and "color" writer for the baseball telecasts.

In the late 1950s, Obojski coached the Detroit Institute of Technology varsity baseball team and has often said since then: "Managing a baseball team, amateur or professional, is one of the most difficult and complex jobs in sport."

He also emphasized that he doesn't want anyone to think that he's just another frustrated ballplayer, for he claims that he had his best season on the diamond in 1955 when he ran playgrounds in Cleveland from the early spring through the late summer and took part in some 200 softball games in that stretch. "I hit 228 homers and drove in over 500 runs that year," Obojski chortled.

Over the years he has written many hundreds of articles on all phases of baseball, in addition to six full-length books: *Bush League—A History of Minor League Baseball* (Macmillan, 1975), *The Rise of Japanese Baseball Power* (Chilton, 1975), *All-Star Baseball Since 1933* (Stein & Day, 1980), *Baseball's Strangest Moments* (Sterling, 1988), *Great Moments of the Playoffs & World Series* (Sterling, 1988), and *Baseball Bloopers & Other Curious Incidents* (Sterling, 1989).

Obojski is also a well-known hobby writer, being credited with a number of books on numismatics and philately, including *Ships and Explorers on Coins* (Sterling, 1970), *An Introduction to Stamp Collecting* (Dover, 1984), *Coin Collector's Price Guide* (Sterling, 1986), *Stamp Collector's Price Guide* (Sterling, 1986), and as co-author of an *Illustrated Encyclopedia of World Coins* (Doubleday, 1970; rev. ed., 1983).

He currently serves as a contributing editor to a wide variety of magazines, including *Collector Editions Quarterly*, *Miniature Collector*, *Dolls Magazine*, *Teddy Bear Review*, *Sports Collectors Digest*, and *Baseball Cards*. He also has been a contributing editor to the *Guinness Book of World Records* and the *Guinness Sports Record Book*.

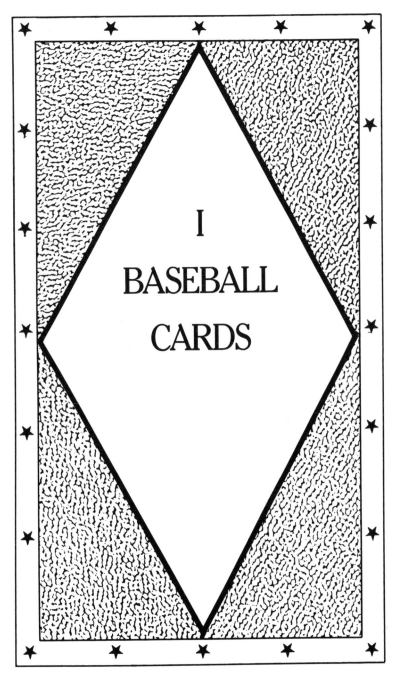

I
BASEBALL
CARDS

Baseball Card Business —and Me

When this writer was a boy back in the late 1930s and 1940s, almost all the kids in the neighborhood collected baseball cards and player autographs.

At that time, however, there were absolutely no generally circulated baseball memorabilia periodicals and no price catalogues being published anywhere. We literally had to do our collecting by the "seat-of-our-pants."

Moreover, we didn't have any card shows where we could buy and sell. We bought our cards one at a time from the local delis and from the corner candy stores—and we further built up our collections by "flipping"—that is, if we were good flippers. (Flipping has been an extremely popular game with youngsters over the decades. The players generally stand 25 to 30 feet away from a wall or abutment, and the one who flips his card closest to that barrier wins the "pot." Expert flippers who can get their cards to "lean" against the barrier can become big winners.)

Nowadays collectors can buy their cards by the box from dealers. For example, the big card manufacturers, like Donruss and Topps, offer sets of cards portraying every player in the major leagues. Donruss' 1990 set consists of 660 cards, one for every player on the 26 teams in the American and National Leagues. Topps' sets, which run to as many as 792 cards, portray every player on the major league *rosters* at the start of each season.

It was really much more of a challenge in the old days to collect complete sets by getting one at a time. The cards cost exactly one cent apiece and that included a stick of bubble gum as big as the card.

No one thought of baseball cards in monetary terms back in the 1930s and 1940s. They were just fun to collect, and if you had used the word "invest" in regard to a card collection, people would think you had a loose screw floating around in your head.

Today, however, many people of all ages do invest seriously in baseball cards—in fact, there are entire companies, companies run by adults, that offer "card investment portfolios."

The company can work out a "tailor-made" plan for the investor. He can kick in, maybe, $100 per month to his portfolio, or if he's a high-roller, he can invest $1,000 per month and more—the company will then use its own discretion in buying cards for the investor that show "appreciation potential." Card prices are tracked like stock prices are tracked by the New York Stock Exchange.

Back when I was 11–12 years old I had the best card collection in the neighborhood, a collection consisting of approximately 2,000 cards, including duplicates. They were all neatly packed into a big box.

Unfortunately, a family member on a cold dark night pitched the whole box into the furnace—and for a reason still unknown to me. That card collection today would easily be worth $50,000—and my entire outlay for it was barely $20. One of the choice specimens in that box, a 1939 Goudey card portraying Ty Cobb, for which I paid exactly one cent, is worth at least $400 to $500 today.

And who knows?—maybe a Don Mattingly or Nolan Ryan card which sells for a few cents today may be worth hundreds of dollars each in the future. When you use the terms "baseball cards" and "investment" together today, people just don't laugh anymore.

The Burdick Collection is housed at New York's Metropolitan Museum of Art. The Museum can be seen here against the background of Central Park and the city's jagged skyline.

Metropolitan Art Museum Houses Greatest Collection of Baseball Cards

"We've got Rembrandts, Titians and Leonardo da Vincis hanging on the walls, but lately it seems as if more persons are interested in looking at our baseball cards than our great paintings," declared a curator at the Print Department of New York City's Metropolitan Museum of Art. The Print Department houses the 400,000-item Jefferson R. Burdick Collection of Trade and Souvenir Cards, of which about half deal with baseball.

The Burdick Collection is open for inspection from 10 a.m. to 12:30 p.m. and from 2 p.m. to 4:45 p.m. Tuesday through Friday (except for holidays). Copies of cards from the Collection measuring approximately 2¾ × 3¾ inches, printed in West Germany, are sold at the Met's souvenir shop.

This magnificent collection was donated to the Metropolitan by Jefferson R. Burdick (1900–63), who as a boy developed a consuming interest for all souvenir cards and maintained that interest for a half-century. Happily, Jeff Burdick made the decision in 1947 to bequeath his entire holding to the Metropolitan. For the remainder of his life he devoted himself to cataloguing the cards and arranging them for easy inspection.

From an artistic viewpoint, the Burdick Collection is prized to the Metropolitan Museum as its largest holding of "pictorial advertising matter and ephemeral printing." The Collection, consisting mostly of American materials, has been supplemented by gifts from Bella C. Landauer of European trade cards, billheads, labels, etc., dating from the late 1600s to the present.

Over the years the Museum has also acquired manufacturers' illustrated catalogues of clothing, furniture, tableware, etc., issued over the years in America and abroad. A. Hyatt Mayor, Curator of the Met's Print Department at the time the Burdick Collection was acquired, observed: "Taken, all together, these collections constitute a continuous record of design, and a history of the pictorial media that business has used to present itself to the public."

This is how baseball cards fit into the general scheme of things at so distinguished an art museum as the Metropolitan.

Besides baseball player cards, the Burdick Collection portrays vaudeville and movie stars, circus performers, political figures, Indians, "Ladies of the White House," "Goddesses of the Greeks and Romans," great buildings, airplanes, animals, flowers, fairy tale characters and flags of the world. There are also extensive

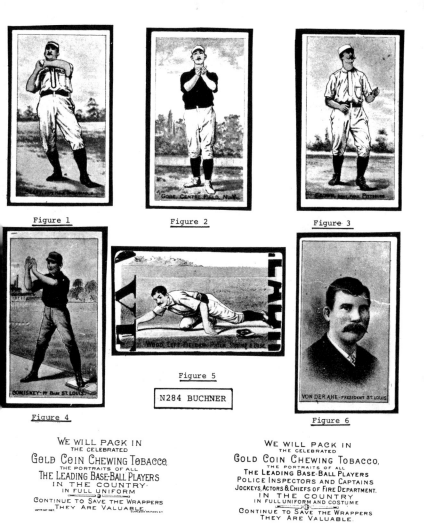

Figure 1

Figure 2

Figure 3

Figure 5

N284 BUCHNER

Figure 4

Figure 6

WE WILL PACK IN
THE CELEBRATED
GOLD COIN CHEWING TOBACCO.
THE PORTRAITS OF ALL
THE LEADING BASE-BALL PLAYERS
IN THE COUNTRY·
IN FULL UNIFORM
CONTINUE TO SAVE THE WRAPPERS
THEY ARE VALUABLE.

WE WILL PACK IN
THE CELEBRATED
GOLD COIN CHEWING TOBACCO,
THE PORTRAITS OF ALL
THE LEADING BASE-BALL PLAYERS
POLICE INSPECTORS AND CAPTAINS
JOCKEYS, ACTORS & CHIEFS OF FIRE DEPARTMENT.
IN THE COUNTRY
IN FULL UNIFORM AND COSTUME
CONTINUE TO SAVE THE WRAPPERS
THEY ARE VALUABLE.

Buchner "Gold Coin Chewing Tobacco" cards, issued c. 1887–88. Shown are: (Fig. 1) Emmett Seery, outfielder, Indianapolis (Indianapolis was then in the National League); (Fig. 2) George Gore, outfielder, New York Giants; (Fig. 3) Tom Brown, outfielder, Pittsburgh Pirates; (Fig. 4) Charles Comiskey, first baseman, St. Louis Browns, American Association (the A.A. was then a major league); (Fig. 5) George Wood, outfielder, Philadelphia Phillies; and (Fig. 6) Chris Von Der Ahe, president, St. Louis Browns. The cards, measuring 1¾ × 3 inches, are printed on thick cardboard. Buchner also portrayed men engaged in other professions. Any Buchner baseball card in superior condition is worth well over $100 today.

arrays of greeting and souvenir cards, playing cards and postal cards.

The myriad of U.S. tobacco companies embroiled in the great "cigarette wars" of the 1880s decided that ballplayers on cards inserted into the packs would stimulate sales of their products more than showgirls and even the great American Indians, and, from that time on, baseball cards have remained an integral part of Americana.

Jefferson Burdick was clearly interested in all things American, as his collection so graphically illustrates . . . and baseball is, of course, something special on the American scene. As Jacques Barzun, the noted professor, once said: "Whoever wants to know the heart and mind of America had better learn baseball."

Jeff Burdick as a person is certainly as interesting as any of his cards. Early in life, arthritis began to stiffen his joints and warp his fingers until finally so simple an act as putting on his hat caused him a painful minute. A. Hyatt Mayor said in an introductory booklet to the Burdick Collection:

"Defying torture, he made his living at the Crouse-Hines Co. in Syracuse by assembling intricate electrical connections for use in mines, flour mills, or wherever an open spark might set off an explosion. Illness probably prevented him from marrying. The energy that he might have put into making a home and bringing up a family, he poured instead into studying insert cards, into editing the *Card Collector's Bulletin*, and writing a series of books on the subject, until he had made himself an expert, whose opinion carried authority far and wide."

Burdick became an active collector in 1910 as a boy of ten. At that time, vintage cards like those from the "Old Judge Cigarettes" series of the 1880s were still rather easily available. In fact, most of them sold for a few cents apiece, while today, of course, they are worth many dollars each.

After more than 35 years of continuous collecting, Burdick began thinking seriously about finding a permanent place to house his treasures, and finally in 1947 he contacted the Metropolitan, and was told that the Museum would like to acquire the entire collection, but suggested that he also contact other institutions which might also be interested. Burdick returned about a

OLD JUDGE CIGARETTES Goodwin & Co., New York.

One of the earliest known baseball cards—an "Old Judge Cigarettes" card, 5 × 7 inches, issued by Goodwin & Co., New York, 1887, portrays Philadelphia Athletics catcher Wilbert Robinson, then at the dawn of his long career. Robinson went on to star for the Baltimore Orioles championship teams of the 1890s, and enjoyed a long career as manager of the Brooklyn Dodgers (1914–31). "Uncle Robbie" gained Hall of Fame election in 1945. The Robinson "Old Judge" card is worth $2,500/3,000.

The John Clarkson Boston Beaneaters "Dogs Head & Old Judge Cigarettes" card, issued by Goodwin & Co., New York City, c. 1888, is a true rarity. Specimens in top grades are worth $3,000 and more. Clarkson pitched only 12 years in the National League, but still managed to post a 328–175 career record and gained Hall of Fame election in 1963. This "Cabinet"–sized card measures 5 × 7 inches.

The Ty Cobb card in the 1910 Sweet Caporal Cigarettes series is valued at approximately $2,500/3,000 for specimens in mint condition. The size of the card is 1½ × 2½ inches. Cobb at this time was only 23 years old, but he had already won three consecutive American batting championships.

COBB, DETROIT

week or so later and told Curator Mayor he strongly felt that the Met had the proper facilities to best care for the hundreds of thousands of cards. An agreement was struck and Burdick effected the first shipment of materials to the Museum in December 1947. During the next decade, additional shipments were made annually until the entire assemblage of cards and related materials was housed in the Met.

Still Jeff Burdick had little time to devote to making his cards suitable for public use, but in 1952 he retired from his Syracuse post, moved to New York City and devoted his full energies to the Collection. He brought from his home his little art nouveau desk and placed it in the only available corner of the crowded Print Department, which almost immediately became the American headquarters of cartophiles from everywhere. Other card enthusiasts came to help him, the chief support being given by Fred Baum.

It had been decided to mount the cards in albums, and by the

Old Judge Cigarette cards, c. 1888, portraying Harry Wright, manager of the Philadelphia Phillies, and Charles Comiskey, player-manager of the St. Louis Browns. These are the "Cabinet" types measuring 4 × 6½ inches. Old Judge Cabinets in top condition are scarce and worth hundreds of dollars each.
(Photos courtesy of Lew Lipset.)

time the monumental job was completed more than 620 albums were filled. The cards were numbered according to Burdick's own *American Card Catalog*. (The final edition which was published under Burdick's direction came out in 1960.)

The albums are near folio size (12½ × 15 inches) and when filled weigh 12 to 15 pounds. Some of the larger items were placed in boxes, with specimens in those boxes having their own catalogue numbers.

A printed list of all albums (and boxes) is available, so a visitor can merely tell a curator which album he wants to see . . . then the visitor can spend as much time as he wants in leafing through. Most cards are pasted down or securely hinged so that normally they will turn with the page without damage.

Burdick himself laid down the basic ground rules governing public inspection. For starters, no ballpoint pens are allowed in the room, and pencils only are allowed for note-taking. No one is permitted to handle a card album and a pencil at the same time because of the chance that a card might accidentally be marked. The number of researchers permitted to use the collection at any one time is always strictly limited to a small handful.

Nevertheless, when a Burdick card enthusiast goes to the Metropolitan's Print Department study room, he is treated much like a guest who visits a friend to see his collection. That's exactly what Jeff Burdick had in mind when he made the donation.

Jeff Burdick set his cut-off point for Topps Baseball cards at about 1955. He admitted that new series were coming out too thick and fast for him by the mid-1950s, and he was content to concentrate on specimens missing from before that period. (The collection has been kept up to date with additional donations, but the Topps series at the Met is by no means complete.)

Curator Mayor reported: "From time to time he would say quite impersonally, 'I may not make it.' But he did. On the 10th of January 1963, he told us at 5 o'clock that he had mounted his last card. As he twisted himself into his overcoat he seemed suddenly tired. When he bade us goodbye, he added, 'I shan't be back.' "

On the next day, Burdick walked from his hotel and was admitted to the nearby University Hospital, where he died exactly two months later. Mayor observed: "The will that drove Jeff Burdick to achieve, drove him on until his work was done. And then it snapped. On first meeting, one felt sorry for this racked frail man, with black-lashed eyes of a haunting gray violet, but pity quickly gave way to admiration—even envy—at his making so much of a bad bargain. All in all, he triumphed more than many."

The richness and vast range of Jefferson Burdick's baseball card collection boggles the imagination. There may be collections today that are larger in sheer number than Burdick's, but none is finer and none contains more rarities and error specimens. No one just starting out today from scratch could hope to match the Burdick assemblage for quality—not even with unlimited financial resources.

Just looking at the pages and pages of the Old Judge Cigarette cards from the 1880s is alone worth a trip to the Metropolitan. You can gaze upon the countenances of stars from baseball's so-called "Stone Age." (that is, from about the time the National League was organized in 1876 until the end of the 19th century). You will see cards picturing "Cap" Anson, Jake Beckley, Dan Brouthers, Pete Browning, Jesse "Crab" Burkett, Bob Caruthers, John Clarkson, Buck Ewing, "Count" Mullane, James "Tip" O'Neill, "Orator Jim" O'Rourke, Jimmy Ryan, "Big Sam" Thompson, "Silent Mike" Tiernan, Charles "Old Hoss" Radbourn, and Jim "Grasshopper" Whitney.

Standard-size Old Judge cards measure $1\frac{1}{2} \times 2\frac{5}{8}$ inches, while the larger size "Cabinets" measure $5\frac{3}{4} \times 8$ inches. The scarcer Cabinets depict such Boston Nationals stars as Dan Brouthers, "King" Kelley and "Old Hoss" Radbourn. As you flip the pages of Burdick's albums, all these big league stars of three and four generations ago seem suddenly to come to life.

Burdick's array of Allen and Ginter Cigarettes "Champions" 1887 "First Series" is also worthy of special note. These cards, measuring $1\frac{3}{4} \times 2\frac{3}{4}$ inches, portray still more of the renowned performers from baseball's hallowed "Stone Age." One of them was Charles (the "Old Roman") Comiskey, star first basemen of the St. Louis Nationals throughout the 1880s, the man who later helped organize the American League and went on to become owner of the Chicago White Sox. Comiskey, a member of the Baseball Hall of Fame (elected in 1939) was the one who revolutionized the style of first-base play by playing off the bag and obliging the pitcher to come off the mound to take throws.

Comiskey's career was marred by the "Black Sox" World Series scandal of 1919. Some baseball historians blame his penurious salary policy for driving his White Sox players to throw games. But on the 1887 Allen & Ginter card, the handsome 28-year-old Comiskey appears as if he doesn't have a care in the world.

Other stars featured this series include: Tim Keefe, New York pitcher; John Montgomery Ward, New York and Brooklyn in-

JOSEPH J. KELLEY
OUTFIELDER OF THE CINCINNATI (N. L.) CLUB

SPORTING LIFE ✕ PHILADELPHIA

Joe Kelley, star National League outfielder, appears on a "Cabinet"-sized card (5 × 7½ inches) issued by Sporting Life *magazine, in 1911. Kelley was a standout hitter for the famed Baltimore Orioles of the 1890s, and went on to play for and manage the Cincinnati Reds in the early 1900s. He gained Hall of Fame election in 1971. The Kelley* Sporting Life *card is valued at from $1,200 to $1,500.*

fielder; Jack Glassock, Indianapolis shortstop; and Charlie Bennett, Detroit catcher.

Most of these players have their careers statistically outlined in Paul Mac Farlane's *Daguerreotypes of Great Stars of Baseball*, published in several editions by *The Sporting News* (affectionately known as "The Dag Book"). Further info on players from the "Stone Age," is, of course, available in Macmillan's *Baseball Encyclopedia*, which is updated and revised on a regular basis.

Photographs of players on many of the classic cards issued by the Old Judge and Allen & Ginter cigarette companies in the 1880s—as well as on most subsequent types issued through the 1890s were indoor "studio shots" rather than field shots. The gladiators of the diamond went to a studio and swung at a ball which was suspended from a string, or made grandiose slides on a thick carpet. In regard to these early cards, Steve Clark, baseball memorabilia historian, commented: "The tremendous charge of flash powder used in photography to provide lighting in those days often gave the players a 'pop-eyed' expression."

Though these studio poses were stilted, the cards were still basically attractive since they were printed on good quality sepia paper. All the cards were included free of charge in tobacco or cigarette pouches, but they were, naturally enough, a bit difficult for youngsters and non-smokers to obtain.

It wasn't until years later that baseball cards were inserted in packages containing gum, candy and other delicacies that appealed to youngsters.

Jeff Burdick compiled a fabulous array of many runs of cigarette cards issued from about 1908 to 1915. These series included Sweet Caporal, Old Mill, Fatima, Mecca, Hassan, Piedmont, Obak, Napoleon and others. The 1908–15 runs can be extremely complicated because one cigarette company may have issued series under different names.

Burdick collected every type and variety of cigarette card of this particular period, from the regular size inserted in the packages to the Cabinet types which generally had to be ordered from the cigarette companies by mail. The Sweet Caporal inserts and the rest of the brands measured about $1\frac{7}{16} \times 2\frac{1}{2}$ inches, while most of the Cabinets were $4\frac{1}{2} \times 7$ inches.

CARRIGAN
Catcher, Boston A. L.

The Ramly Turkish cigarette cards of 1909 rank as one of the most interesting of the early 20th century tobacco series due to their ornate gold and white borders. Bill "Rough" Carrigan, a Boston Americans catcher, went on to manage the Bosox to World Series championships in 1915–16 while still remaining on the active roster. Actual size of the cards is 1½ × 2½ inches.

Issued as premiums for Turkey Red, as well as Old Mill and Fez cigarettes, the so-called "Turkey Red" cards are unusually popular because they are big and portray most of the outstanding diamond stars of the early 1900s . . . moreover, the color lithographs were extremely well done.

These are the 1910–11 Cabinet cards, listed as "T-3" in Burdick's catalogue. According to the instructions on the cigarette packs, the coupons were to be mailed to the "Baseball & Athletic Picture Department, Drawer S, Jersey City, N.J." This was a tough way to get the Cabinets cards, but enterprising youngsters often could scrounge up hundreds of coupons and get lots of the big cards in return.

These Cabinet cards reveal a great deal about baseball players of the early 1900s. Ty Cobb, for example, is shown gripping the bat with his hands 3 to 4 inches apart . . . this grip is unseen today. Ty Cobb used it effectively for complete bat control and wound up with a stratospheric lifetime batting average of .367.

In examining the cards, you will find that other top hitters of the day also utilized the hands-apart grip, for one, the star outfielder Tris Speaker, then with the Boston Red Sox. Later on, however, Speaker pulled his hands together.

Other renowned players depicted on these large-size cards include: Mordecai "Three-Finger" Brown, Chicago Cubs; Sam Crawford, Detroit; "Bad Bill" Dahlen, Brooklyn; Bobby Wallace, St. Louis Americans; Frank Chance, Chicago Cubs; Eddie Collins, Philadelphia Athletics; Norman "Tabasco Kid" Elberfeld, Washington; Hal Chase, New York Americans; and John McGraw, New York Giants manager.

The cards are outstanding because they give clear facial expressions and a wealth of other graphic details. For example, on the Mordecai Brown card, we can clearly see that most of the pitching star's right index finger is missing. Though he was called "Three Finger," Brown actually had a thumb as well on that right pitching hand. Brown, who won 208 major league games from 1903 to 1916, having his best years with the powerful Chicago Cubs, had lost that index finger as a boy, when he was feeding field corn into a chopper on an Indiana farm. The loss of a gripping part of his hand gave him a natural "sinker" pitch that

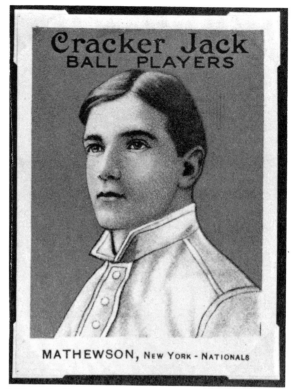

MATHEWSON, New York - Nationals

The "Cracker Jack" baseball cards issued in 1914–15 are extremely popular due to their bright red backgrounds and because they portray so many Hall-of-Famers. The Christy Mathewson card is #88 from the 1915 series.

acted like a knuckle ball, dropping down sharply as it crossed the plate.

The cards show us that the players of the immediate pre-World War I era wore fielders' gloves that appear to be primitive by today's standards. These gloves, dubbed the "motorman's mitt," they weren't all that much bigger than a player's hand. For that reason, players, even the best of them, committed errors by the gross. Bill Dahlen, who was supposed to be a pretty good fielding shortstop, made exactly 1,063 errors in his big league career, while John McGraw as a third baseman rolled up a miserable

.899 fielding percentage in his career. With better gloves, those stats wouldn't have been so horrific.

None of the players portrayed on these pre-World War I cards are seen wearing beards, mustaches or long hair. Though a minority of players from the 1880–1890 period wore goatees and mustaches, any type of facial hair pretty much went out of style before the end of the century. It wasn't until the mid-to-late 1960s that gladiators of the diamond felt free to grow lots of facial hair as a symbol of masculinity.

(In the particular Burdick album containing the "Turkey Red" and related cards, non-baseball materials are also mounted. There are Cabinets of similar size, for example, showing vaudeville and movie stars, including Lillian Russell, Maude Adams and Tom Mix.)

Rare Honus Wagner
Sweet Caporal Card

Most valuable of all cigarette cards is the Honus Wagner from the Sweet Caporal series (catalogued by Burdick as "T-206"), with the great shortstop being included in a set showing members of the 1910 Pittsburgh Pirates team. The Wagner card is rare because this charter Hall of Fame member disapproved of smoking and didn't want his portrait to be associated with tobacco. The tobacco company almost immediately withdrew his card from circulation with very few specimens being extant, perhaps fewer than 30.

In a Burdick album the Wagner card is mounted under clear plastic in the center of a page including Sweet Caporal cards showing six other members of the 1910 Pirates. "After we show this album, we always double check to make sure the Honus Wagner card is still in place," a Print Department staff member told us.

Honus Wagner, shortstop for the Pitts-burgh Pirates in the early 1900's, noted for his base stealing, was elected to the Hall of Fame. Today he is equally renowned for the baseball card issued in 1910 and called back by the ciga-rette company because Wagner, a non-smoker, objected. Wagner never received any money for it, but the card sold for $10,000 a generation ago and now is quoted at $100,000 or more.
(Card supplied by Tom Miceli and B&E Collectibles, Thorn-wood, N.Y. Photo by V. J. Holland)

Burdick's Album No. #314 contains over 2,400 early candy and gum cards, numbered #E 1-E 137 in his *American Card Catalog*. Period covered in this outstanding album is before 1910 into the mid-1920s, and again an array of non-baseball cards is included ("Military Heroes," "Boxing Champions," "Jockeys," etc.).

"E" cards first appeared in the late 19th century, but they really started to come into their own in about 1910, when gum and candy companies realized how successful tobacco companies were in promoting their products through use of collector's cards. Again, you see a a panoramic view of ballplayers—from the "spear carriers" to the bright stars—of several generations through examining these cards.

In the American Caramels "Baseball Stars" series, c. 1910 (un-numbered cards measuring 1½ × 2¾ inches, we have players like "Turkey Mike" Donlin, Eddie Grant (National League infielder who was killed in action in France on Oct. 5, 1918 while serving with the A.E.F.), Ed Walsh (the spitball king who won 40 games for the Chicago White Sox in 1908), and Cy Young (the 511-game winner who was finishing up his long career with Cleveland and Boston).

All standard baseball card catalogues today use the basic Burdick numbering system . . . and if a collector wants to *see* all the cards in the "E" series, for example, he can do so at the N.Y. Metropolitan Museum of Art. Moreover, Burdick gathered together all the minor and error varieties which are not catalogued in detail anywhere else.

Error Cards

Really amazing are the many errors found in the various "E" series cards, mostly in the spelling of player names. In an E-120 Ross Youngs, the New York Giants outfielder has his name inscribed without the "s" at the end of his name. Youngs scintillated in the majors for only a decade (1917–26) before illness cut him down. (He died on Oct. 22, 1927, just short of his 31st birthday.) Youngs, who gained Hall of Fame election in 1972, was praised by his manager, John McGraw, as "My Greatest Outfielder."

On an E-210 (York Caramel Co., *c.* 1921–22). Roger Peckinpaugh, Washington shortstop, has his first name spelled "Rogers." No doubt the card writer was thinking of Rogers Hornsby, the great National League slugger of the 1920s.

On another E-210, we'll see Joe Dugan's name misspelled as "Duggan." "Jumpin' Joe" Dugan, starred for the New York Yankees as a great fielding third baseman in the Roaring Twenties.

On an E-220 (National Caramel Co., *c.* early 1920s card), Jim Bagby's name for some unknown reason is twisted to "Bagbyk." That's about the worst butchery of a name ever. Bagby, a crafty right-handed pitcher who enjoyed his best years with the Cleveland Indians from 1916–23, rolled up a monumental 31–12 record in 1920, plus a World Series victory against Brooklyn.

Max Bishop
"ATHLETICS"

ZEENUT
SERIES
PC LEAGUE
LEARD
VENICE

The Metropolitan Museum of Art reproduced these "very scarce" baseball cards through a West German printer for sale at its gift shop. Carl Hubbell's given name is spelled "Karl," the German way. The "Wild Bill" Leard (Zeenuts) card, c.1912, is of particular interest. Leard, who spent his prime years as a good fielding second baseman and base-stealing wizard with the Oakland Oaks, played in only three major league games (with the Brooklyn Dodgers in 1917). The Zeenuts cards produced commercially 1911–1939 by the Collins-McCarthy Candy Co., San Francisco, was the longest-running card series until Topps cards began pouring forth in 1951.

Karl Hubbell
"GIANTS"

The Bagby spelling error was soon corrected . . . and we'll see that Burdick places the error card alongside the corrected version.

Hobbyists owe Jeff Burdick a debt of gratitude for placing and so brilliantly arranging his magnificent collection in the Metropolitan Museum of Art, so that all true collectors can have an opportunity to examine it. If a collector wants to get full mileage from this unique assemblage, he should allow himself more than one day for the pleasant chore of viewing the cards, photos and related items. Even a week of mornings and afternoons would not be nearly sufficient to see everything.

Insofar as error cards are concerned, virtually every major series issued during the past century contains a myriad of errors of one type or another. Most baseball hobby publications employ writers who specialize in error cards and report on them in detail.

"Eight Men Out" Card Series

The 1988 "Black Sox" movie based on Eliot Asinoff's 1963 book "Eight Men Out," relates the story of how the Chicago White Sox threw the 1919 World Series, one of the darkest events in all baseball history.

As part of the promotional campaign for the film, Orion Pictures Corporation, in conjunction with Pacific Trading Cards, Inc., turned out a high-quality series of 110 cards. The cards depict all of the film's major actors, plus actual photographic portraits of all the key White Sox and Reds players who participated in that infamous World Series that rocked the very foundations of professional baseball.

The complete "Eight Men Out" series was originally priced at $10, but because of its continued popularity, the full set now sells at a premium considerably over the issue price.

Eddie Cicotte
Pitcher

Eight Men Out

Dickie Kerr
Pitcher

Eight Men Out

George "Buck" Weaver

Eight Men Out

"Kid" Gleason

Eight Men Out

JOE JACKSON

Joe Jackson Reinstatement Unlikely Despite Petitions, So Cards Suffer

"Shoeless" Joe Jackson took $5,000 from gamblers to "throw" games in the 1919 Black Sox World Series scandal. Then, with a change of heart, he tried unsuccessfully to give the money back, and went on to hit .375 in the Series, with a record-tying 12 hits, including 3 doubles and a homer in the 8 games, making 15 putouts without an error.

What his backers fail to mention is that he allowed a couple of catchable fly balls to drop near him, and he made some lame throws from left field following base hits.

Petitions calling for Jackson's reinstatement have been circulating at card shows across the country, but these attempts to exonerate the slugger have proved to be futile since all recent Baseball Commissioners have thus far turned down all requests to "clear the record."

For example, in early June, 1989, the legislature of South Carolina (Jackson's home state) passed a resolution asking for Joe's reinstatement, but the then Commissioner Dr. Bart Giamatti turned down the request saying that he did not "wish to play God with history."

The Joe Jackson situation is similar to that of Pete Rose. If Pete and Joe don't get into the Hall of Fame, prices for their memorabilia will remain flat, or decline. Shoeless Joe at first signed his contracts and letters with an "X", but as he matured he did learn how to write and his signature is usually a strong and clear one.

Pat Tabler holds the record for highest batting average (.514, 38 for 74) with the bases loaded and for RBI of 93. He began in 1981 as first baseman-outfielder with the Chicago Cubs, then Cleveland Indians and KC Royals. In 1990 he was acquired by the NY Mets.

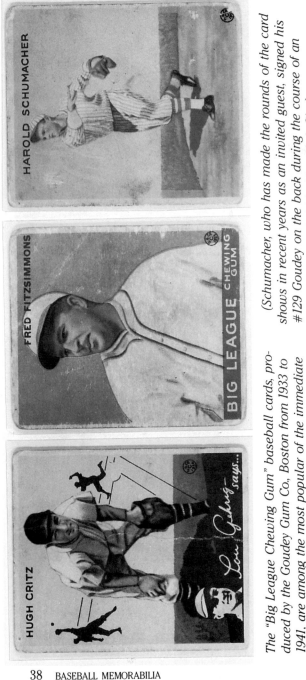

The "Big League Chewing Gum" baseball cards, produced by the Goudey Gum Co, Boston from 1933 to 1941, are among the most popular of the immediate pre-World War II issues. The player portraits consist of drawings based on photos. Shown are three cards from the 1934 series, all portraying members of the pennant-winning 1933 New York Giants: Hugh Critz, second baseman; and pitchers Fred Fitzsimmons and Hal Schumacher.

(Schumacher, who has made the rounds of the card shows in recent years as an invited guest, signed his #129 Goudey on the back during the course of an early 1990 event held in New York City.)

Cards of the pre-World War II era are generally quite scarce because so many of them were consigned to "waste paper" drives during the course of the war.

HUGH CRITZ

NEW YORK GIANTS

"Up among the leaders in National League fielding last year was Hugh Critz, a Starkville, Miss., boy who crashed into professional baseball in 1920 with Chattanooga of the Southern League and has been playing second base ever since. He entered the National League via the Cincinnati gate and has been with the Giants since 1930. He finished 1933 as one of the two best fielding second basemen with an average of .982.

"As a boy Hugh was keen on pitching, but when he got into professional baseball he just gravitated to the infield and has been there ever since. He is 5 feet, 8 inches tall and weighs around 150 pounds."

This is one of the 1934 Series of pictures of Big League Baseball Stars. Collect the entire series.

BIG LEAGUE
CHEWING GUM
GOUDEY GUM CO.   BOSTON
Made by the originators of
INDIAN GUM

— No. 13 —

FRED FITZSIMMONS

NEW YORK GIANTS

Knuckle ball pitcher. Last year won 11 games and lost 11. Came to the Giants in 1925 from the Indianapolis club of the American Association where he had won 14 games and lost 6, and has been in the big show ever since.

Raises chickens when not playing ball.

Born at Mishawaka, Ind., in 1901 and began his baseball playing career there. Played three years in Muskegon, Mich., then went to Indianapolis in 1922.

Bats and throws right-handed. Is five feet 11¼ inches tall and weighs around 190 pounds.

This is one of a series of 240 Baseball Stars

BIG LEAGUE
CHEWING GUM
GOUDEY GUM CO.   BOSTON
Made by the originators of
INDIAN GUM

HAROLD SCHUMACHER

NEW YORK GIANTS

One of the pitching aces of the New York Giants, a right hander, 6 feet tall and weighing around 180 pounds.

Signed by the New York Giants after leaving St. Lawrence University in 1931; sent to Bridgeport and Rochester for more experience that year. Won five games and lost six for the Giants in 1932, being used to a large extent as a relief pitcher. One of the Big Four in the Giants' sensational showing in 1933.

Born in Hinckley, N. Y. in 1911.

Has plenty of smoke on his fast ball.

This is one of a series of 240 Baseball Stars

BIG LEAGUE
CHEWING GUM
GOUDEY GUM CO.   BOSTON
Made by the originators of
INDIAN GUM

The text on the back of the Schumacher card is not entirely correct since "Prince Hal" did not "leave" St. Lawrence U. in 1931. He attended winter sessions while playing in the spring and summer and graduated in June 1933. All of Schumacher's teammates traveled up to the university campus in Canton, N.Y. to view the graduation ceremonies. This sojourn proved to be a "good luck charm" for the Giants as they went on to win both the N.L. pennant and the World Series.

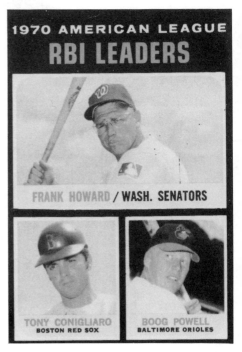

(Left) The Bowman Gum Co. in 1948 produced the first major American baseball card series since the beginning of World War II.

The company continued to manufacture cards through the early 1950s, but Bowman was eventually bought out by Topps, who consolidated its position as the most important sports card issuer. Shown is the Don New-combe Bowman card, series of 1952. Within the two years prior to 1990 the entire Bowman series has been re-issued in facsimile form.

(Right) "Combo," or multiple portrait cards, have long been popular with collectors. This 1971 Topps "Combo" portrays the three RBI leaders in the American League for 1970: Frank Howard, Tony Conigliaro and John "Boog" Powell.

1970 AMERICAN LEAGUE
RBI LEADERS

FRANK HOWARD / WASH. SENATORS

TONY CONIGLIARO
BOSTON RED SOX

BOOG POWELL
BALTIMORE ORIOLES

George Steinbrenner: Baseball Card Collector

George M. Steinbrenner III, the former principal owner of the New York Yankees—his group bought the team in 1973—was the only chief executive who was able to overshadow his players. His do-or-die mania infected all things. Anything less than a World Series victory at the end of the season was considered a disgrace.

Though Steinbrenner became known as one of baseball's freest spenders on the free-agent player market, he still maintains an air of frugality in his personal financial affairs. Perhaps he acquired this quirk from his father George M. Steinbrenner II, who owned the Kinsman Transit Co., based in Cleveland, Ohio, a firm that operated five or more freighters on the Great Lakes.

Though Dad Steinbrenner was a wealthy man, he told his son early on, "No allowance!" Instead, he bought young George chickens. Out of those chickens came the eggs that George sold to buy baseball cards (as well as James Fenimore Cooper novels), and very quickly the boy had the best baseball card collection in the neighborhood.

Steinbrenner's wide-ranging baseball card collection contained all the major series of the late 1930s and early 1940s, including the Goudeys, Diamond Stars, Batter-Up and Play Balls. While he was enamored of all the big league stars of the day, he had a penchant for collecting cards portraying standout members of the Cleveland Indians: e.g., Earl Averill, Hal Trosky, Mel Harder, Joe Vosmik, Bob Feller, Johnny Allen, Rollie Hemsley and Bruce Campbell.

Curiously enough, Steinbrenner favored playing football over baseball, and after his collegiate gridiron days were ended (Williams College, Class of 1952), he went on to become an assistant coach at Northwestern and Purdue Universities.

In 1990, Steinbrenner was forced to resign as the controlling "General Partner" of the Yankees on orders from Baseball Commissioner Fay Vincent. Nevertheless, Steinbrenner in 18 years unquestionably garnered more newsprint mentions than any other chief executive in baseball history.

JOHN BERTRAND (JOCKO) CONLAN

Umpire Cards

It's actually more difficult for an umpire to gain election to the Baseball Hall of Fame than a player since only six arbiters have been so honored: Tom Connally, Bill Klem, Cal Hubbard, Bill Evans, Jocko Conlan and Al Barlick.

Happily enough, numerous umpires have been depicted on various baseball card series. All HOF umps are, of course, included in the Hall of Fame "Gallery" series, as well as in the Steele-Perez series of multicolored cards done for the HOF.

Shown here is a top-caliber Jocko Conlan card issued by T & M Sports, Inc. Jocko gained HOF election in 1974.

Rare Athletes

Deion Sanders

Deion Sanders is one of the rare contemporary athletes, like Bo Jackson, who has been able to compete in the major leagues in two sports, baseball and football. Sanders played parts of the 1989 and 1990 seasons for the New York Yankees as an outfielder, and then in the latter parts of each of those years he joined the Atlanta Falcons of the National Football League where he scintillated as a cornerback.

Sanders (a 1989 Heisman Trophy winner while at Auburn), in fact, electrified the sports world in 1989 when he slammed a home run for the Yankees in Seattle on Sept. 6 and, with a quick uniform change, ran a punt return for a dazzling touchdown for the Falcons on Sunday, Sept. 10—a homer and a touchdown within the same week!

The only other athlete to turn a major league home run and touchdown trick within the same week was Jim Thorpe who performed the feat twice: with the Cincinnati Reds and the Canton Bulldogs (American Professional Football Association) in Sept. 1917, and with the Boston Braves and Canton Bulldogs in Sept. 1919.

Both Sanders and Bo Jackson have appeared on various series of baseball and football cards. Deion Sanders is shown here on his 1989 "Score" rookie card.

Sanders' and Bo Jackson's paths crossed in a dramatic way on July 17, 1990 at Yankee Stadium. Jackson, playing for the Kansas City Royals, had slammed out 3 homers in his first 3 at-bats, and then in the 6th inning Sanders connected for a line drive-inside-the-park home run. Jackson, playing left field, lunged for the ball vainly and in doing so fell and injured his shoulder with the result that he was forced to spend nearly 6 weeks on the disabled list.

Painting by Larry Eisenstein

Mark McGwire, Oakland Athletics home run slugger, is portrayed on a 1987 card done in the manner of the famed National Chicle "Diamond Stars" series of 1934–36. This "Repli-Card," one of a series, was produced by Krause Publications as an insert for its monthly Baseball Cards *magazine.*

Pittsburgh and New York A.L. only pitcher to win pitching championship in both leagues 1901 and 1902 A.L. and 1904 N.L.
AN EXHIBIT CARD

The Jack Chesbro "Exhibit Card" was issued shortly after "Happy Jack" was elected into Baseball's Hall of Fame in 1946. The caption isn't quite correct, however, since Chesbro won pitching percentages while with the National League's Pittsburgh Pirates in 1901–02 and with the American League's New York Yankees in 1904. Chesbro compiled an amazing 41–12 record for the 1904 Yankees, and no other 20th century major league pitcher has won more games in a single season. Chesbro's lifetime record over 11 seasons (1899–1909) is 198–132 (.600 pct).

A trio of Topps cards. . . . contemporary issues show us that all current major leaguers (1990) wear batting gloves, a phenomenon unknown a dozen or so years ago. Most players won't even remove their gloves when they sign autographs. Steve Kemp's card (opposite page) is particularly interesting because it details on the back Kemp's outstanding record as a collegiate player.

(See opposite page)

Many current baseball card manufacturers favor showing full-length player portraits, sometimes also with career totals. This is New York Mets' shortstop Kevin Elster's 1989 "Upper Deck" card.

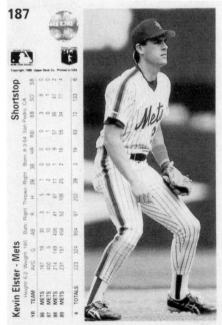

Care and Preservation
of Baseball Cards

True baseball card collectors are sticklers for condition, and, therefore, it's highly advisable that hobbyists *not* keep their packs of cards together with rubber bands, the way some of us did when first starting out years ago.

There's a big difference in value, for example, between a Very Good (VG) and a Mint (MT) rated card, and rubber band marks can create real havoc in regard to condition.

All cards of value should be placed within special clear plastic individual holders, or within clear plastic album sheets. The plastic itself should be of such quality that it does not tarnish the cards in any way. Cards should not be touched, for even the slightest handling can wear away the finish. For a "Mint" rating, the card must retain the original finish.

By the same token, baseball cards and stamps should not be hinged down into an album . . . they must be placed in special protective holders—and the same principle holds true for cacheted philatelic covers.

Moreover, autographed baseballs should be placed in special plastic ball holders that can be set down on a library shelf.

The weekly *Sports Collectors Digest* and the monthly *Baseball Cards Magazine* are filled with advertisements from dealers who specialize in all types of accessories for baseball memorabilia collectors.

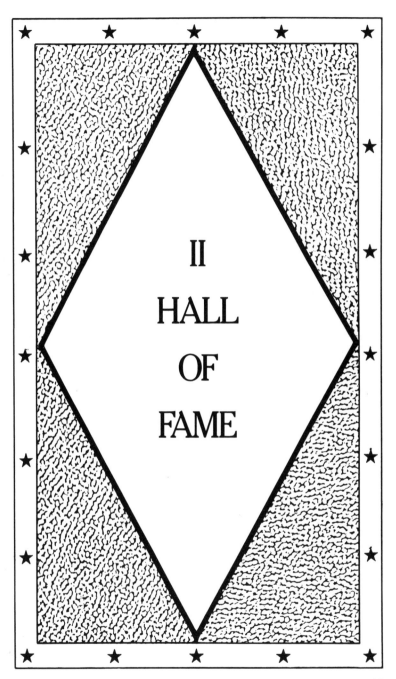

II

HALL

OF

FAME

Baseball Memorabilia: The Baseball Hall of Fame in Cooperstown, NY, celebrated its 50th anniversary on June 10, 1989 by opening the new Fetzer-Yawkey Building, bringing its display area to more than 70,000 sq. ft. Annual paid attendance runs to more than 350,000. The HOF's newest building program calls for an expansion of the Baseball Library, with the expected costs to total some $8 million. The new facility is to be called the "A. Bartlett Giamatti Memorial Library" in honor of the late Baseball Commissioner.

National Baseball
Hall of Fame
and Museum

Cooperstown, New York is a Mecca for the baseball memorabilia collector: the world-renowned Hall of Fame. Why Cooperstown?

The Mills Commission was set up in 1905 to determine the origin of the game of baseball, and submitted its final report in 1908 after a three-year investigation. The report stated in part:

"The first scheme for playing baseball, according to the best evidence obtainable to date, was devised by Abner Doubleday at Cooperstown, N.Y. in 1839."

The Mills Commission took its name from Colonel A. G. Mills, who played baseball before and during the Civil War and who went on to serve as the fourth president of the National League (1882–1884). The six other members of the Commission were prominent men who had been associated with baseball and/or athletics in one way or another: Morgan G. Bulkeley, former governor and then U.S. senator from Connecticut, who acted as the N.L.'s first president in 1876; Arthur P. Gorman, U.S. senator from Maryland, former player and ex-president of the National Baseball Club of Washington, D.C.; Nicholas E. Young of Washington, D.C., a longtime player and later fifth president of the N.L. (1884–1902); Alfred J. Reach of Philadelphia and George Wright of Boston, both well-known sporting goods entrepreneurs and two of the most famous 19th century ballplayers; and James E. Sullivan, president of the New York-based Amateur Athletic Union.

Catalyst for the formation of the Mills Commission was Albert Goodwill Spalding, one of the game's pioneers, who in 1876 founded A. G. Spalding & Bros., a major sporting goods firm that has survived to this day. Spalding, who strongly believed that baseball developed strictly from American origins, became con-

Tobacco and Gum Card Display: This very large exhibit consists of over 900 different baseball cards and includes samples of every type in the Hall of Fame's collection, dating back to 1887.

cerned following publication of a magazine article by Henry Chadwick, who contended that the sport evolved from the English game of rounders. Chadwick (1824–1908), a pioneer baseball writer, originated the box score and compiled baseball's first authoritative rule book.

During its lengthy deliberations the Mills Commission was literally deluged with communications on the subject. The testimony of Abner Graves, an elderly mining engineer from Denver, Colo., in support of Abner Doubleday as the true founder of baseball was to figure prominently in the commission's conclusions.

Graves contended that he and Doubleday attended school together in Cooperstown. Doubleday later was appointed to the U.S. Military Academy at West Point, graduating in 1842 at the age of 23. Subsequently, he served in the Mexican, Seminole and Civil

It's always October at the Hall of Fame's World Series Room. Housed here is the greatest assemblage of memorabilia relating to the "Fall Classic": press pins, programs, ticket stubs from famous games, photos, score sheets, autographed balls, video presentations, etc. At right is a cardboard cutout depicting Oakland's Joe Rudi making a spectacular, backhanded catch of Cincinnati's Denis Menke's drive against the leftfield wall that assured the A's of victory over the Reds in Game 2 of the 1972 World Series. Oakland prevailed in that Series 4 games to 3.

Wars. As a captain he fired the first gun for the Union Army at Fort Sumter, S.C., in 1861.

In a series of letters to both Spalding and members of the committee, Graves claimed to have been present in 1839 when Doubleday—at Cooperstown—made changes in the popular game of "Town Ball," which involved 20 to 50 boys and young men out in a field attempting to catch a ball hit by a "tosser" using a long flat bat. According to Graves, Doubleday used a stick to mark out a diamond-shaped field in the dirt. His other "refinements" ostensibly included limiting the number of players, adding bases (hence the name "baseball"), and the concept of a pitcher and catcher.

While the Mills Commission pretty much accepted Graves' version of how baseball originated, there were some doubters from the very beginning. Some said that Doubleday had never even been to Cooperstown—and certainly not in 1839 when he supposedly modified Town Ball into baseball for he was already at West Point as a second-year man. Doubleday had been born at Ballston Spa., N.Y., a small town some 60 miles northeast of Cooperstown, but there is no evidence to suggest that he ever attended schools in Cooperstown, as Graves indicated.

Despite the reservations expressed concerning the conclusions of the 1905 Mills Commission report, the nation's sports fans did come to believe that Abner Doubleday did, indeed, "invent" the game of baseball at Cooperstown in 1839.

By the end of the Civil War, Doubleday had attained the rank of major-general and retired from active service in 1873. He had fought with particular distinction at Gettysburg and in 1917 a bronze statue of General Doubleday in full military uniform was unveiled at Gettysburg. He died at Mendham, N.J., on Jan. 26, 1893, at the age of 74.

The "Doubleday Baseball"

Early in 1935, an ancient-looking misshapen and undersized baseball was found in the attic of a farmhouse in the tiny cross-roads village of Fly Creek, located about three miles from Cooperstown. The farmhouse and the trunk in which the ball was found had belonged to Abner Graves.

The cover of the obviously homemade ball had been torn open, revealing stuffing of cloth instead of the wool and cotton yarn which comprise the interior of the modern baseball—but it did have a stitched cover.

Also found in the trunk with the baseball was a packet of

yellowed letters explaining that the spheroid had been used by youngsters playing on the Phinney pasture (now the site of Doubleday Field, Cooperstown) during the Abner Doubleday era.

This spectacular find obviously strengthened the Mills Commission report rendered 27 years earlier. The beat-up and battered old spheroid became known as the "Doubleday Baseball." The ball and accompanying documents were placed on display in a local shop soon after the find and attracted an enormous amount of attention in Cooperstown. Townspeople flocked to see the exhibit, and it was then that Stephen Carlton Clark went into action. He bought the ball for $5, had it mounted, and then displayed it together with other examples of baseball memorabilia at the Otsego County Historical Society, Cooperstown.

Clark was a prominent Cooperstown businessman, historian, philanthropist and enthusiastic collector of early Americana who had amassed considerable wealth through his association with the Singer Sewing Machine Co. He visualized that the "pedigreed" ball, busting at the seams, would serve as the centerpiece for a permanent display that would keep Cooperstown forever mindful of its baseball heritage.

To that Historical Society exhibit he added his own collection of paintings and prints, including a renowned drawing showing Union prisoners playing baseball at Salisbury Prison during the Civil War, and the original oil painting of a championship baseball match at the Elysian Fields in Hoboken, N.J., in 1846.

Then Clark assigned a member of his management staff, Alexander Cleland, to scour the country for other authentic baseball relics to add the growing collection. Cleland, a stocky, red-faced little Scotsman, with the broad burr of the Highlands in his speech and the missionary ardor of a John Knox in his soul, adopted the project as a personal challenge.

In the course of a year he visited baseball people from coast to coast and back again. From the National League office he obtained the original Temple Cup, emblem of major league baseball supremacy in the 1890s.

Clark Griffith contributed a large collection of photos from Washington, while J. Taylor Spink, publisher of *The Sporting News*, sent voluminous files of documents, official papers and

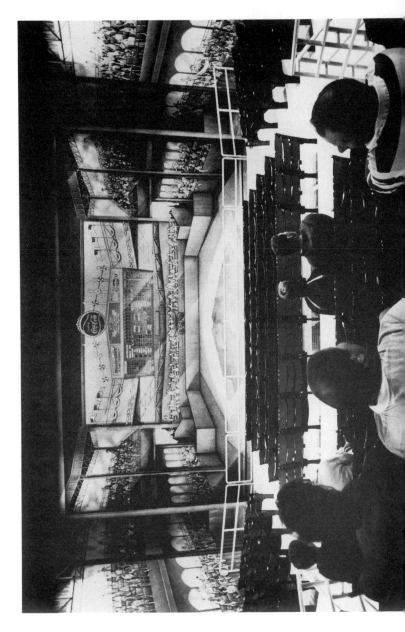

(Caption on next page)

photos that were to become the nucleus for the Hall of Fame library. Other significant contributions of first-rate historical material came from Connie Mack, William M. Wrigley, Mrs. Christy Mathewson and Mrs. John McGraw.

Stephen Clark and Ford Frick Join Forces

The idea for a Hall of Fame—where baseball's greatest players would be enshrined—came from Ford Frick, National League president, with the first elections for the HOF being conducted in 1936. Ty Cobb, Honus Wagner, Babe Ruth, Walter Johnson and Christy Mathewson were the first five players to be elected.

And since Stephen Clark was working on his museum at this time, his project melded beautifully with that of Ford Frick into the formation of the National Baseball Hall of Fame and Museum.

In his autobiography, *Games, Asterisks and People* (New York: Crown Publishers, Inc., 1973), Frick, who had gone on to serve as baseball's commissioner for 14 years (1951–65), paid tribute to Clark:

"He proposed the organization of the National Baseball Museum, Inc., for the purpose of collecting and preserving pictures and relics reflecting the development of the National Game from the time of its inception, through the ingenuity of Major-General Doubleday in 1839 to the present." Frick wrote further:

"Furthermore, Clark said he would personally take responsibility of erecting in Cooperstown a suitable building to house

(Opposite page) In this simulated ballpark, a spectacular multi-media presentation is shown continuously. The theatre, located in the Baseball Hall of Fame's Fetzer-Yawkey Building, holds 200 people.

LUCIUS BENJAMIN APPLING
CHICAGO A.L. 1930-1950
A.L. BATTING CHAMPION IN 1936 AND 1943.
PLAYED 2,218 GAMES AT SHORTSTOP
FOR MAJOR LEAGUE MARK.
HAD 2,749 HITS.
LIFETIME BATTING AVERAGE OF .310.
LED A.L. IN ASSIST 7 YEARS.
HOLDS A.L. RECORD FOR CHANCES
ACCEPTED BY SHORTSTOP 11,569.

such a collection in perpetuity and he invited Organized Baseball to join with him in establishing the first museum in American history devoted entirely to a sport, baseball."

The dedication of the Baseball Hall of Fame and Museum took place on schedule on June 12, 1939, to coincide with the celebration of the sport's centennial. This is what Ford Frick had to say about that June day in Cooperstown more than a half century ago:

". . . Twelve thousand fans that day crowded the little village and heard Judge Landis deliver an inspiring dedication speech.

LOUIS CLARK BROCK
CHICAGO N.L., 1961-1964
ST. LOUIS N.L., 1964-1979
BASEBALL'S ALL-TIME LEADER IN STOLEN BASES WITH
938. SET MAJOR LEAGUE RECORD BY STEALING OVER
50 BASES 12 TIMES AND N.L. RECORD WITH 118 STEALS
IN 1974. LED N.L. IN STOLEN BASES 8 TIMES. COLLECTED
3,023 HITS DURING 19 YEAR CAREER AND HOLDS
WORLD SERIES RECORD WITH .391 BATTING AVERAGE
IN 21 POST-SEASON GAMES.

Never before or since have so many great personages of base-ball, players and officials alike, joined together in one place to honor baseball. The President of the United States extended an official greeting. Postmaster-General James Farley supervised the sale of a special commemorative stamp recognizing baseball's centennial as a national game. It was baseball's finest hour, perhaps never again to be duplicated by any sport, any time, anywhere."

For starters, all of the living Hall of Famers were present at that June 12, 1939 event (all told, 25 players and executives had gained HOF membership up to that point).

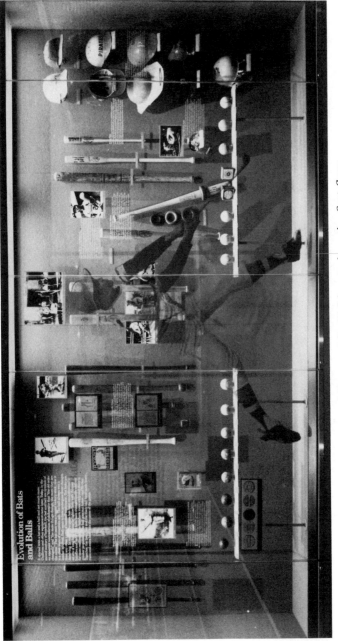

"Evolution of Bats and Balls," located on the first floor of the new Fetzer-Yawkey Building, is one of the most popular exhibits at the Baseball Hall of Fame and Museum.

Another singular event at those ceremonies was a minor league all-star game played at Doubleday Field (located only a block away from the baseball museum).

Doubleday Field was originally built in the late 1920s, but it was entirely rebuilt and modernized according to major league specifications, with a seating capacity of nearly 10,000. Since 1940, Doubleday Field has been the site of the annual "Hall of Fame Game," where teams from the American and National Leagues face each other on the day following the HOF induction ceremonies. The stands are always jammed to capacity for this event. A portion of the proceeds from the sale of tickets for this clash go to the support of the Hall of Fame and Museum.

Ford Frick also wrote in his autobiography: "What started as a single colonial brick building has grown into a huge complex. A new wing has been added to the museum—a wing almost twice as large as the original building. A cathedral-like Hall now houses the Hall of Fame, separate and apart from the museum."

A library has been constructed (completed in 1968), dedicated to the writers, the artists and the cartoonists who have contributed so much to the growth of the game. . . . That library today is the repository of the greatest array of records, historic documents, pictures and authentic books and articles ever assembled on a single American sport subject in the history of the nation. . . . New material is added continuously to keep information up to date."

Bear in mind that Frick wrote these words some 20 years ago. Since 1973 the Hall of Fame and Museum has continued to grow dramatically in size. In 1982, a three-year expansion and renovation program requiring an expenditure of more than $3 million was completed.

The Hall of Fame and Museum celebrated its 50th anniversary on June 10, 1989 with an array of ceremonies climaxed with the dedication of the new Fetzer-Yawkey Building that increased the complex's size by about one-third. This new building was named in honor of John E. Fetzer, chairman of the board of the Detroit Tigers, and Jean R. Yawkey, president of the Boston Red Sox, whose generous contributions helped make this major museum expansion possible.

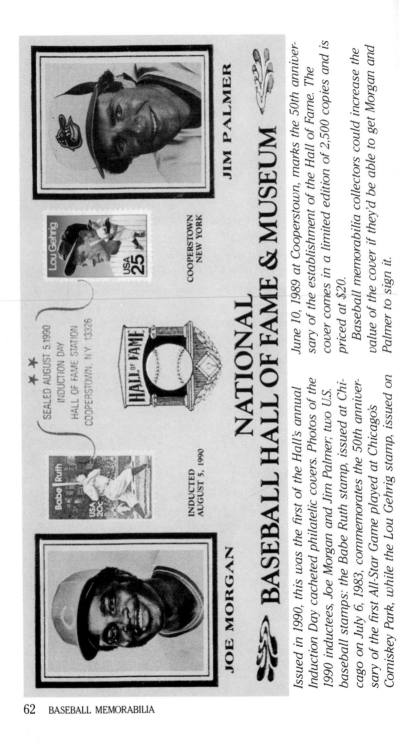

NATIONAL
BASEBALL HALL OF FAME & MUSEUM

JOE MORGAN

JIM PALMER

COOPERSTOWN
NEW YORK

SEALED AUGUST 5.1990
INDUCTION DAY
HALL OF FAME STATION
COOPERSTOWN, N.Y. 13326

INDUCTED
AUGUST 5, 1990

Issued in 1990, this was the first of the Hall's annual Induction Day cacheted philatelic covers. Photos of the 1990 inductees, Joe Morgan and Jim Palmer; two U.S. baseball stamps: the Babe Ruth stamp, issued at Chicago on July 6, 1983, commemorates the 50th anniversary of the first All-Star Game played at Chicago's Comiskey Park, while the Lou Gehrig stamp, issued on June 10, 1989 at Cooperstown, marks the 50th anniversary of the establishment of the Hall of Fame. The cover comes in a limited edition of 2,500 copies and is priced at $20.

Baseball memorabilia collectors could increase the value of the cover if they'd be able to get Morgan and Palmer to sign it.

The Fetzer-Yawkey Building includes the new Grandstand Theater where visitors are entertained by a stirring multi-media presentation utilizing state-of-the-art technology. This presentation, which has many similarities to a Cinerama-type movie, is intended to create a thrilling ballpark-type atmosphere as the fans begin to enter the theater.

A. Bartlett Giamatti, the late baseball commissioner, who presided at the Hall of Fame's 50th anniversary ceremonies, made his own personal observations on the new HOF theater: "As I began walking up the ramp, I heard the sounds of a ballpark, and I wanted to start running because fans were cheering like crazy and I thought I was missing a bases-loaded homer, a steal of home or some other exciting play."

The theater contains exactly 200 seats, the slat ballpark type, but it seems like more because the entire room is so large. There are scores of ballplayer vignettes in the film with the most exciting—at least in the writer's estimation—being that of an outfielder using the bleacher wall as a kind of springboard to make a sensational one-handed catch to rob the batter of what seemed like a sure homer.

Ted Spencer, HOF Curator, indicated that the outfielder making this acrobatic catch plies his profession in the Japanese professional leagues!

So, okay. . . . Abner Doubleday had nothing to do with baseball, never set foot in Cooperstown and Abner Graves had a fuzzy and unreliable memory.

And so, okay most responsible baseball historians regard Alexander Cartwright, who patterned the game upon English predecessors, the true father of baseball. After all, it was Cartwright, an engineer, who ingeniously located the bases 90 feet apart and established nine innings as a game and nine players as a team. He provided for three outs per side, set an unalterable batting order, and eliminated throwing the ball at a runner to retire him.

And it was Cartwright who organized baseball's first team— the New York Knickerbockers in 1845. And in the first "match" on record, Cartwright's Knickerbockers on June 19, 1846 beat the "New Yorks" 23–1 at the Elysian Fields, a summer resort in Hoboken, N.J. Consequently, writers such as Jerry Izenberg of the

New York Post believe that the Hall of Fame should have been located in Hoboken rather than in Cooperstown. Nevertheless, a plaque has been placed in Hoboken marking the spot where the Knickerbockers and New Yorks met on that historic June 19, 1846 date.

At the same time, however, Cartwright is duly honored as a baseball founder since he was voted into the HOF at Cooperstown in 1938. Cartwright was associated with the Knickerbockers through 1848 and gained a reputation as one of the best players of his era. Starring as an infielder, outfielder and catcher, he had no trouble hitting. The curveball or "crooked pitch" wasn't invented until 1869—WIlliam "Candy" Cummings is given credit for this nasty invention. (Cummings achieved HOF recognition in 1939.)

No doubt there was at least a form of baseball activity going on in Cooperstown in the late 1830s and early 1840s, particularly the playing of "Town Ball." Some mythmakers contend that Cartwright and Doubleday were teammates, but the two never met.

The Hall of Fame itself recognizes that pinpointing the origins of baseball is an incredibly difficult task and that many questions surrounding the game's early development may never be answered adequately. In this respect the HOF released an official statement which appeared in their *Yearbook* for 1988. The statement reads:

"From time to time over the years, various critics have challenged the speculation on Abner Doubleday, although most of the original documentation was lost in a fire in 1916. Abner Graves' reliability as a credible witness has been questioned and Doubleday's diaries, surprisingly, made no mention of baseball. . . . and to further complicate matters, still others claim that there were two Abner Doubledays. Many of these contradictory theories have been well-documented by their proponents. Whatever may or may not be proved in the future concerning Baseball's true origin is in many respects irrelevant at this time. If baseball was not actually first played here in Cooperstown by Doubleday in 1839, it undoubtedly originated in a similar rural atmosphere. The Hall of Fame is in Cooperstown to stay; and at the very least, the village is certainly an acceptable symbolic site."

Appropriately enough, the 3-cent stamp issued by the United States on June 12, 1939, to commemorate the centennial of baseball features in its central vignette being played by a group of youthful players in a rural setting. We see in the background a house, barn, schoolhouse and a church.

Featuring the vignette of a sandlot ball game, this 3¢ stamp was released on June 12, 1939 at Cooperstown, N.Y., to commemorate the centennial of baseball in America.

Strong Leadership at Hall of Fame

Since its inception more than a half-century ago, the National Baseball Hall of Fame and Museum has been administered by a series of talented executives and specialists, beginning with Stephen C. Clark. Clark, who obtained his A.B. from Yale and a law degree from Columbia, served in the U.S. Army during World War I, saw duty in France during the final six months of the conflict and attained the rank of lieutenant colonel. He became director of several major corporations and was also instrumental in founding the Farmers Museum in Cooperstown, serving for many years as president of that museum.

After Clark's death in 1960 at the age of 78, he was succeeded as HOF president by Paul Kerr, an astute administrator who for years had played an active part in planning and implementing the Clark family projects in the Cooperstown area. After Kerr retired in 1977, Edward W. Stack, museum secretary, succeeded him as president, a position Stack still holds.

New Materials Keep Pouring In

- A western cowboy hat worn by Dizzy Dean during the height of his baseball broadcasting career.
- A grandstand seat from Pittsburgh's old Forbes Field described as "used, but in good condition."
- The base stolen by Tim Raines of the Montreal Expos on August 13, 1987, at Montreal. (Raines' 500th career stolen base.)
- The batting helmet worn by Bill Mazeroski of the Pittsburgh Pirates and the bat he used when he slammed his historic home run in the seventh game of the 1960 World Series to topple the New York Yankees.

These and scores of other artifacts have been either donated or loaned to the Baseball Hall of Fame Museum within the past year or two.

Peter Clark, HOF registrar, keeps track of all museum acquisitions. Each is documented with the name of the donor and the date of acceptance.

William Guilfoile, HOF associate director, called Mazeroski's bat "one of baseball's most treasured artifacts."

Gene Kirby, a longtime baseball broadcaster and major league club official (mostly with the Montreal Expos), is the one who donated the cowboy hat Dizzy Dean used while doing play-by-play accounts in his inimitable way. As an announcer, Dizzy had a tongue that was often as sharp as his fastball. When the pace of the game he was announcing slowed down a bit, he often broke out into song, with his favorite number being "The Wabash Cannon Ball." He sang a bit off-key, of course.

The grandstand seat from Pittsburgh's Forbes Field (torn down after Three Rivers Stadium opened in 1970) is the "folding style," dark blue with iron and wooden slats, 31 inches high, 15 inches wide and 13½ inches deep.

Grandstand seats from old ballparks have a strong following among collectors. For example, individual seats from Yankee Stadium (almost completely torn down in the early 1970s to make way for a new ballpark) have commanded prices of $700 to $1,000 and more at public auctions.

Anything is collectible. One donation made to the HOF recently consists of five bulbs and two circuit chips from the original Houston Astros scoreboard in the Astrodome. These components, dating back to the mid-1960s, were saved when the old scoreboard was removed in 1988.

The Tim Raines stolen base, manufactured by Rawlings, a major sporting goods producer, carries the inscription in red paint, "Tim Raines/500/87-08-13." For insurance purposes the base (a second base sack) is valued at $300.

Silver Medals

The Baseball Hall of Fame in 1989 issued a silver-proof medal commemorating its 50th anniversary, a medal designed by Frank Gasparro, former Chief Engraver at the U.S. Mint. The medal's obverse shows the facade of the Hall of Fame Museum in Cooperstown, N.Y., while the reverse depicts a symbolic "Hall of Famer" at bat against the backdrop of a baseball diamond, while the inscription around the edge has the names of the five charter HOF inductees: Christy Mathewson, Babe Ruth, Ty Cobb, Walter Johnson and Honus Wagner. The number "25" at the batter's right signifies that the medal has a face value of $25 for HOF Museum entrance fees. The medal is available at the Baseball Museum's gift shop.

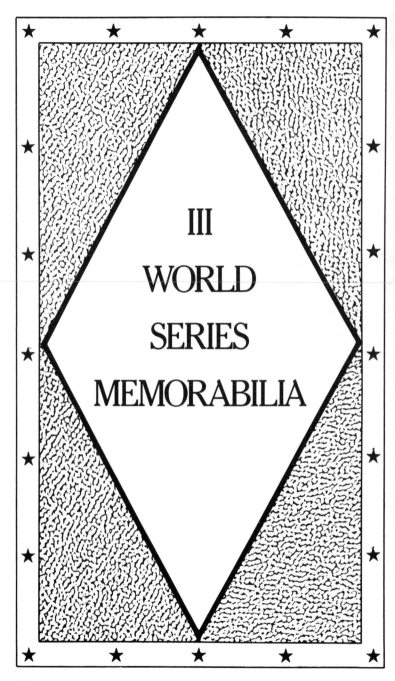

III

WORLD

SERIES

MEMORABILIA

World Series Collectibles

Baseball's premier event for nearly 90 years now, has been the World Series and any type of memorabilia directly connected with the "Fall Classic"—anything from ticket stubs, official programs and press pins to autographed baseballs, uniforms and player rings—carries a premium value.

The first modern World Series was played in 1903 between Pittsburgh of the National League and Boston of the fledgling American League. The National League, or "Senior Circuit," had been formed in 1876, while the American League, or Junior Circuit," was not organized until 1901. However, the first actual "World Series" had been played in 1885.

That year, the Chicago White Stockings, pennant winners of the National League, and the St. Louis Browns, champs of the American Association (then considered a major league) clashed in a best-of-seven post-season series to determine the world champions of baseball. After seven games the series ended in a deadlock, with each team winning three games and tying one in nine innings. Apparently, neither team thought the series was important enough to play longer and determine a clear-cut winner.

This "Stone-Age" World Series was loosely organized; the number of games and general ground rules changed from year to year, reflecting the pliable nature of the leagues and the game itself. Still, the series continued to be played through 1890. It was suspended simply because the American Association foundered and folded in 1891.

For the next decade, the National League reigned as baseball's only major circuit, but a pent-up demand remained among the fans for some type of playoff. Consequently, the "Temple Cup Series," a best-of-seven series between the first-place and second-place N.L. teams was inaugurated in 1894.

The playoff was the brainchild of William C. Temple, former president of the Pittsburgh N.L. franchise, who donated a $500 silver trophy for the winner. The winning team received a 65 percent share of the net profits from the gate receipts, while the losers received the rest. The New York Giants surprised the pennant-winning Baltimore Orioles in the inaugural Temple Cup play by sweeping them in four straight games.

In 1895, the champion Orioles again bowed to the second-place team, the Cleveland Spiders who won 4 of the 5 games, but the Orioles came back the next year to knock out the second-place Spiders in 4 straight. While the Orioles finished second in 1897, they knocked off the champion Boston club 4 games to one. That was the last of the Temple Cup Series.

Examples of memorabilia from the World Series of the 1880s and the Temple Cup Series of the 1890s are scarce, indeed, but it's still possible for the serious collector to pick up a few items. Forget about getting one of the silver Temple Cups, because they never seem to come on the market. Stephen C. Clark, founder of the National Baseball Hall of Fame and Museum, did manage to get an original Temple Cup back in the late 1930s when he was assembling materials for exhibit. The elaborate and ornately engraved cup is prominently displayed on the Museum's main floor.

Happily, though, many 19th-century tobacco cards contain references to the Gaslight Era series. For example, first baseman Charlie Comiskey (known as the "Old Roman") was a standout for St. Louis of the American Association in four World Series (1885–88), banging out 43 hits in 38 games. These tidbits of info can be found on his Old Judge cards and other classic cards of a century ago.

Comiskey's teammates on those great St. Louis Browns teams of the 1880s included speedy third baseman Arlie Latham (nicknamed "The Freshest Man on Earth") and hard-hitting outfielder James "Tip" O'Neill. They also starred in those ancient World Series, and they had their achievements recorded on cigarette cards. On Oct. 18, 1886, against Detroit, Tip O'Neill became the first player to hit two homers in a World Series game.

Cy Young, star righthander for the old Cleveland Spiders, almost single-handedly derailed the Baltimore Orioles in 1895 Temple Cup play when he beat them three times without a defeat, allowing them only 7 runs in 27 innings. Young also pitched for Boston in the first modern World Series in 1903; his two victories were a key factor in the Boston Pilgrims' five-games-to-three margin over the Pittsburgh Pirates. Young's post-season achievements are cited on many of his contemporary baseball cards.

The National League was humiliated, to say the least, by Pittsburgh's ignominious loss to Boston in that inaugural World Series. The N.L. thought itself far superior to the A.L., which it considered to be an inferior upstart. Upstart or not, the Pilgrims whipped the Pirates handily.

In 1904, the New York Giants, led by manager John J. McGraw (who had played third base for Baltimore in the 1895–96 Temple Cup Series), dominated the National League, rolling up a spectacular 106–47 record and finishing 13 games ahead of the Chicago Cubs.

In 1904, in the American League, the pennant race went right down to the wire, with Boston again coming in ahead of the tough New York Highlanders by a mere game and a half.

McGraw and the Giants' owner John T. Brush, however, for complicated reasons, refused to meet the Pilgrims in a World Series, and none was played.

John McGraw's Giants breezed to another pennant in 1905, as they compiled an outstanding 105–48 record and finished 9 full games ahead of the Pirates. There was no way that the Giants could duck meeting the A.L. pennant-winning Philadelphia Athletics in a World Series.

The A's, under Manager Connie Mack, who had also taken the 1902 flag (before the World Series began), had wound up with a 92–56 record in 1905 to edge the Chicago White Sox by 2 games.

The ill feelings of McGraw and John T. Brush toward A.L. President Ban Johnson (a major reason for the scuttling of the '04 Series), drifted into the background. Brush actually became the World Series' biggest booster, and devised a code that made the post-season playoff compulsory for the pennant winners of both leagues.

The so-called "Brush Rules" are in large part still in effect to this day. Among other things, they govern the selection of umpires, makeup of rosters, printing of tickets, division of revenues—and they also lay down the guidelines as to dates and locales of Series games.

In that historic 1905 Series, the Giants bested the A's, 4 games to 1, as their star righthander Christy Mathewson, a great screwball artist, hurled three consecutive shutouts, including a 6-hit blanking in the decisive fifth game.

The 1905 battle firmly established the World Series as a national institution. The intensity of the rivalry between the two leagues and the enormous publicity the World Series received was an elixir for the game. Baseball prospered and expanded because of the World Series. All teams placed getting into the World Series as their chief goal, and the furious pennant races that resulted caused the modest wooden parks with their limited seating capacity to be replaced by new stadiums of brick, concrete and steel in the major league cities.

And since the divisional playoffs were instituted in both major leagues in 1969, the buildup for the World Series has become even greater.

World Series Programs

Some sort of official program was produced for every World Series from 1903 to the present, and a complete collection of these programs in decent condition would be worth a small fortune. Programs were turned out for the Temple Cup series of 1894–97, and prices for the originals are literally out of sight. They almost never appear on the market, but in recent years good quality reprints were made and quickly snapped up by collectors.

Keep in mind that there were almost always two sets of World Series programs printed each year (until recent times), one by each team. For instance, there's a 1936 World Series program printed by the New York Giants, but there's also an entirely different program that year produced by the New York Yankees.

Since 1974, though, only a single World Series program has

World Series programs are highly prized collectibles. A vintage specimen like the 1930 St. Louis Cardinals vs. Philadelphia Athletics at St. Louis program (more accurately called a "score card") will sell for $600 to $800 if it's in top condition. Most of the other World Series programs shown on this page are currently valued at from $300 to $500.

been produced each year, and is distributed exclusively through Major League Baseball Promotion Corp.

Many hobbyists believe that programs are the most interesting of all World Series collectibles because they contain such a wide variety of interesting information—they're filled with statistics, player biographies, team histories, information tables, photos, artistically designed covers, etc.

One of the most historic and famous programs is from the 1917 New York Giants vs. Chicago White Sox series (which the Giants won 4 games to 2). The cover features a smiling portrait of President Woodrow Wilson in a first-ball ceremony. In good condition a program like this can sell for $2,500 to $3,000.

Among other outstanding programs is the one produced for the New York Yankees vs. New York Giants Series which was played entirely at the Polo Grounds, the home then of both teams. (Yankee Stadium wasn't completed until 1923). This program, a joint effort of the two teams, portrays on its front cover the two managers, John McGraw of the Giants and Miller Huggins of the Yankees. It'll take two or three thousand bucks to get a copy of this program in decent condition. Remember that most of them were thrown out once the series concluded, and the number of extant originals is very low.

All of the classic World Series programs have been reprinted by RDO Publications (2829 Toyon Drive, Santa Clara, Calif. 95051). The reprints are handsome and absolutely authentic, yet clearly marked as reprints. It's impossible to top the real thing, but the originals cost anywhere from several hundred to several thousand dollars a copy. The reprints, which cost about $15 each, are a very attractive alternative.

World Series Tickets

The most obvious evidence of a World Series is a ticket. And, according to Scott Forst, a Huntington Station, N.Y. dealer who specializes in World Series collectibles, there's a very simple rule of thumb regarding "Fall Classic" tickets and their values.

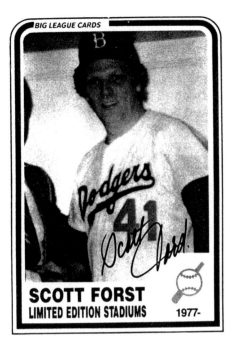

BIG LEAGUE CARDS

SCOTT FORST
LIMITED EDITION STADIUMS   1977-

*Scott Forst, who has operated his Limited Edition baseball mem-
orabilia business for more than a dozen years, had his own
bubble-gum card made up and it doubles as his business card.
Forst, who saw minor league service as an outfielder with the
Brooklyn Dodgers Class D Pony League farm club at Hornell, N.Y.,
in the late 1950s, specializes in Brooklyn Dodgers collectibles. The
#41 Dodgers jersey he wears once belonged to Clem Labine, who
pitched for the Dodgers (both in Brooklyn and Los Angeles) for
more than a decade beginning in 1950.*

"Those World Series tickets commanding the highest prices
are the ones that deal with the truly outstanding games," Forst
said. Forst indicated that in most cases we'll have to be satisfied
with the ticket stubs (or "rain checks"), but at the same time he
emphasizes that examples of full tickets for various historic
games do occasionally crop up on the market—and sell for
premium prices.

Among the hottest ticket stubs and/or full tickets are from the first game of the first modern World Series (at Boston, Oct. 1, 1903); the fifth game of the 1905 World Series (at New York, Oct. 14), when Christy Mathewson pitched his third straight shutout against Philadelphia; the fifth game of the 1920 Series (at Cleveland on Oct. 10), when Indians' second baseman Bill Wamby (Wambsganss) pulled off an unassisted triple play against the Brooklyn Dodgers and Indians outfielder Elmer Smith belted the first grand-slam homer in Series history; the third game of the 1932 World Series (Oct. 1, at Chicago's Wrigley Field), when Babe Ruth slammed his famed "called-shot" homer off Cubs' right-hander Charlie Root; the fifth game of the 1956 World Series (Oct. 8 at Yankee Stadium), when the Yanks' Don Larsen hurled a perfect no-hit game against the Brooklyn Dodgers; and the sixth game of the 1977 World Series (Oct. 18 at Yankee Stadium), when New York's Reggie Jackson hit three successive homers against Los Angeles Dodgers pitching.

Forst (like most other dealers) doesn't like to be pinned down in quoting prices for tickets from highly dramatic World Series games, but he maintains that prices for pre-1940 tickets may run into many hundreds of dollars when they're available. Condition is a major factor in determining the price—the better the condition, the higher the price.

"Years ago collectors pasted their World Series tickets down into albums, and thus we'll find residue on their reverses," Forst said. "That cuts down on their value. But if it wasn't for those pioneering collectors we wouldn't have nearly as many vintage tickets around today."

Press Pins and Autographed Series Balls

This 1911 Philadelphia Athletics World Series press pin, with ribbon attachment, is worth several thousand dollars. In that 1911 Series, Connie Mack's Athletics defeated John McGraw's New York Giants, 4 games to 2.

Collecting World Series press pins has become a more and more popular segment of the hobby. First of all, the press pins have always been issued in limited quantities since they're really intended to be given out to members of the media only. For that reason they can bring very strong prices, and are quite likely to increase in value. Secondly, they're quite attractive, especially when in top condition. Finally, they're prized as nostalgic items.

In the early days of the World Series, the press pins were

relatively crude celluloid buttons, but over the years the designs became more sophisticated and almost always featured the team logos. They became even more artistic after World War II when Balfour, the Attleboro, Mass., jewelry maker, began turning out most of these annual issues.

In getting a line on price for World Series press pins, collectors can check the myriad of dealer ads in such periodicals as *Baseball Cards*, *Sports Collectors Digest* and *Baseball Card News*. For example, the 1928 St. Louis Cardinals (vs. New York Yankees) press pin has been quoted recently in the $1,200/$1,300 price range, while the very scarce 1938 Chicago Cubs (vs. New York Yankees) specimen has been selling in the $3,000 price range. Collectors who want complete sets are going to need both money and ingenuity to reach their objectives.

Fortunately, press pins issued within the past dozen years or so are not that outrageously priced. For example, the 1983 Baltimore Orioles and Philadelphia Phillies press pins (issued separately) are being quoted in the $50/$60 price range. Still, considering how relatively few were made, who knows how expensive they'll be ten years from now?

Baseballs autographed by World Series winning teams are naturally highly desirable items. A ball autographed by members of the great 1927 New York Yankees World Series champions commands a boxcar price today. The most prized signatures on such a ball are those of diamond titans, Babe Ruth and Lou Gehrig.

A ball signed by members of the 1930 World Champion Philadelphia Athletics is nothing to be sneezed at either. Hall of Fame signatures on a ball of this magnitude include Connie Mack, Al Simmons, Jimmie Foxx, Mickey Cochrane and Lefty Grove.

World Series jewelry constitutes another major collecting area. Within the past half-century or so, players, managers and coaches on World Series winners have been receiving specially made rings, exquisite pieces of jewelry crafted with gold and precious stones. In recent years, each player of a World Series winner has had his name inscribed on his ring. And, yes, sometimes a member of a championship team needs money in a hurry and sells off his ring to a dealer or collector. Reggie Jackson may not need extra money all that much, but his 1978 New York Yankees World Series ring came on the market recently and commanded a price in the $5,000 range. At the same time, we must realize that players often give their rings to a family member or friend and often the latter—and not the player himself—sells off the World Series jewelry.

World Series memorabilia collecting is a fascinating and far-ranging segment of the hobby. But if a collector wants to become properly inspired, he must visit the World Series Room at the National Baseball Hall of Fame and Museum in Cooperstown, N.Y. The museum contains absolutely the greatest assemblage of materials on this planet, relating to every aspect of the Fall Classic. The HOF Collection literally boggles the imagination. But there's nothing that says you can't assemble a collection that will stimulate your imagination as well.

Vintage World Series press pins are eagerly sought after by collectors. This 1926 New York Yankees specimen is currently estimated at about $2,500/3,000.

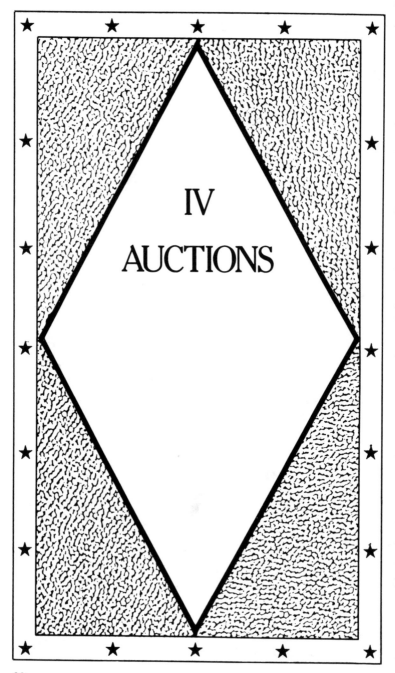

IV

AUCTIONS

Memorabilia Auction Prices for Collectibles

Most major auction houses in the United States now regularly conduct public sales that feature significant sections of baseball memorabilia. These auction houses include Christie's and Sotheby's based in New York, and Butterfield & Butterfield's based in San Francisco.

However, Guernsey's, one of the newer major auction houses and headquartered in New York City, has almost literally "lapped the field" in regard to public baseball collectible sales.

For example, in regard to Guernsey's "The Sporting Auction" conducted at "Passenger Pier 90" along the Hudson River on April 28–29, 1990, the more than 2,000 lots of material in the sale, with the majority of them baseball items, sold for more than $2 million, making this, perhaps the largest auction of sports collectibles ever offered in the U.S.

Top realization for a single lot at the Guernsey's sale was the $110,000 paid for a complete set of the 320 "Cracker Jack" baseball cards issued in 1914–15. The cards are extremely popular among collectors because of their attractive red backgrounds and because several dozen Hall of Fame ballplayers are portrayed in the set, including Grover Cleveland Alexander, Frank "Home Run" Baker, Mordecai "Three-Finger" Brown, Ty Cobb, Eddie Collins, Miller Huggins, Walter Johnson, Connie Mack, Christy Mathewson, John McGraw, Edd Roush, Tris Speaker, Honus Wagner and Zack Wheat.

Lou Gehrig items brought very strong prices. For starters, a game-used Gehrig bat, and autographed to a fan in 1938, brought a winning bid of $28,600, making this the most expensive baseball bat in history.

Lou Gehrig's blue enamel and diamond-studded 1939 All-Star Pin, measuring barely one square inch, was hammered down for $41,600. Lou Gehrig removed himself from the Yankees lineup on

Lou Gehrig's famed #4, which had previously been on display at Yankee Stadium, together with Gehrig's name plaque which had hung on "Columbia Lou's" locker, received a bid of $40,000, but that sum wasn't sufficient to meet the consignor's "reserve."

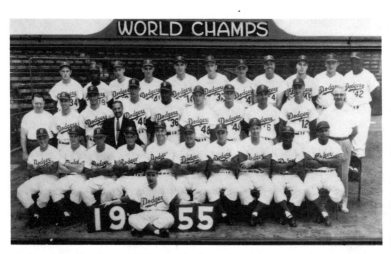

A Brooklyn Dodgers 1955 world championship team photograph fetched $3,850. The original framed photo had been displayed at the offices of old Ebbets Field.

An official American League baseball signed to "Billy Rogers" by Babe Ruth and dated November 29, 1939 sold for $4,400 at Guernsey's "The Sporting Auction."

May 2, 1939, after having played in a record 2,130 consecutive regular season games . . . and the American League honored "Columbia Lou" by naming him as honorary captain of the A.L. All-Stars that year. Gehrig received the pin in a special ceremony before the start of that year's "Midsummer Classic" played on July 11 at Yankee Stadium. Gehrig sat on the bench for the entire game as the A.L. won 2–1.

Babe Ruth's famed number #3, taken from one of his game-used uniforms, sold for $19,800. The magical #3, on a piece of fabric measuring 11 × 13 inches, had previously been on display at the old Yankee Stadium.

A single signature Mel Ott official National League ball, having

Pete Rose's 1963 Cincinnati Reds #14 rookie baseball jersey (McGregor, size 44) sold for $8,250 at Guernsey's April 28–29 "The Sporting Auction." The jersey achieved this high price despite the removal of the lettering "Rose" from the back.

A Mel Ott single signature official National League baseball, c. 1940s, stamped with the facsimile signature of League President Ford Frick, sold for $6,600 at Guernsey's New York City, April 28–29 "The Sporting Auction." The ball has been partially shellacked to preserve the signature.

the facsimile signature of N.L. President Ford Frick, fetched $6,600.

An official National League ball signed by the late baseball Commissioner Bart Giamatti and Pete Rose, two bitter adversaries, was knocked down for $3,300, more than triple the estimate.

An official National League ball signed by ex-president Richard Nixon sold for $412.50.

"Prices for baseball collectibles being sold at auction are reaching all-time highs," observed Barbara Mintz, a Guernsey's vice president. "Even the ladies are getting into memorabilia collecting," she added.

American League Championship rings given out to individual members of the 1969 Baltimore Orioles are valued at about $2,000/2,500. Players in need of funds often put up their prized souvenirs and trophies for sale.

Highlights of Christie's 1990 "Sports Memorabilia" Auction

Featured was a large autographed photo portrait of Babe Ruth, 13 × 10½ inches. The black-and-white print was inscribed in black ink "To my friend Jack Lawton from 'Babe' Ruth, Dec. 15th 1931," and sold for $1,870, well over estimate.

At the same auction an official American League baseball, c. 1934 signed by Ruth on the "sweet spot" and also signed by 7 of Ruth's teammates (Sam Byrd, Lou Gehrig, Earle Combs, Dixie

Walker, Lefty Gomez, Ben Chapman and Jimmie Deshong) brought a substantial $2,200, nearly triple the estimate.

The Yankee Stadium Opening Day Program, April 18, 1923, featuring cover portraits of the Yankees' co-owners, Col. Jacob Ruppert and Col. T. L. Huston, brought $770, approximating the estimate. Inside the program are photos of all the Yankee players including Babe Ruth, Joe Dugan, Herb Pennock, George Pipgras and Bob Shawkey. The program is in excellent condition except for a crease on the cover.

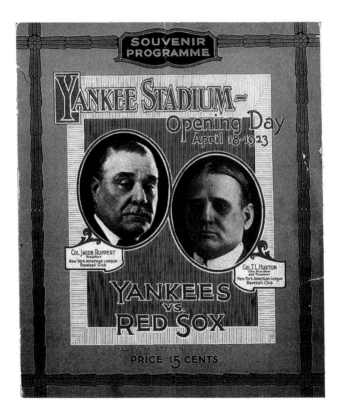

Tins from "Bambino Smoking Tobacco," c. late 1920s, are rarely found in presentable condition, and are valued at $1,000/1,500. A silhouette of Babe Ruth in a batting pose is featured on the tobacco tin's face.

This official National League baseball, signed by some 20 members of the 1945 New York Giants, sold for $880 at a Sotheby's New York auction in June 1989. The signatures include those of Player-Manager and Hall-of-Famer Mel Ott, Bill Voiselle, Charley Mead, Rube Fischer, Van Lingle Mungo and Buddy Kerr.

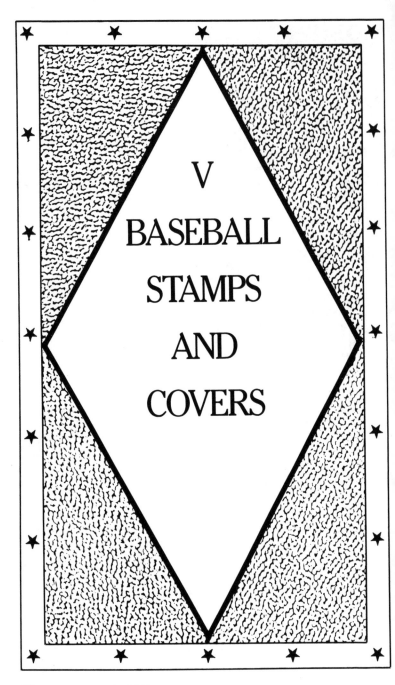

V

BASEBALL

STAMPS

AND

COVERS

Postage Stamps of Many Nations Depict Baseball Players

Since the Philippine Islands issued the first ever baseball stamp in 1934, more than 50 countries around the world have collectively produced well over 1,000 varieties of postage stamps.

Baseball as a "World Game" was launched by Albert Goodwill Spalding (1850–1915), a member of Baseball's Hall of Fame, who also ranks as the game's first authentic goodwill ambassador. Spalding became the first professional pitcher to win more than 200 games. He posted a glittering 252–68 record with the Boston Red Stockings of the National Association and with the Chicago White Sox of the National League from 1871 through 1877.

In the summer of 1874, he took his Boston Red Stockings and the Philadelphia Athletics on an exhibition tour through England. Then, in 1888, he organized a world tour. The Chicago White Sox (by this time he was their owner) and an all-star team from the National League's seven other clubs played exhibition games in England, Ireland, France, Egypt, Ceylon, Australia and Hawaii. The tour took nearly six months, ending in March 1889, just in time to start the new National League season. Spalding believed that once people in other nations saw baseball played by professionals, the game would quickly sweep the globe.

It didn't happen quite that way, especially because of the continued popularity of other sports, including cricket and soccer. In recent years, however, baseball has been catching on in many parts of the world, with this phenomenon being graphically illustrated through the large numbers of stamps featuring baseball. All this would have made Spalding very happy.

Many baseball stamps pertain to international tournaments. For example, the 1972 Nicaragua souvenir sheet of four values publicizes the 20th International Baseball Championships staged

Ajman, one of the United Arab Emirates, issued this series in 1969.

at the capital, Managua, from Nov. 15th to Dec. 5th of that year. The four labels list the 23 "countries" that participated in those championships: Germany, Aruba, South Africa, Brazil, Costa Rica, Canada, Cuba, Colombia, South Korea, El Salvador, the U.S.A., Guatemala, Honduras, The Netherlands, Italy, Japan, Mexico, Nicaragua, Peru, Puerto Rico, Panama, the Dominican Republic and Venezuela.

In the future a good many baseball stamps will be released in conjunction with the International Summer Olympic Games. Baseball was a regularly scheduled event for the first time in Olympics history in 1984 when the diamond game was played as a demonstration sport at the 23rd Olympiad staged at Los Angeles. All games in '84 were played at Dodger Stadium. Baseball again was contested as a demonstration sport at the 24th Olympiad held at Seoul, South Korea in 1988. Baseball will become a full-fledged medal sport at the 25th International Olympiad to be conducted at Barcelona, Spain, in 1992. The '92 Summer Games should cause a profusion of baseball stamps to be issued.

Cuba fields strong baseball teams in most international competitions, including the Olympic Summer Games—and at the same time Cuba has been one of the world's most prolific issuers of baseball stamps. Since 1957 Cuba issued nearly 100 major varieties in all. However, because of the U.S. embargo on trade with Cuba, proclaimed by President John F. Kennedy on Feb. 7, 1962, the importation from any country of stamps of Cuban origin, used or unused, is prohibited. Consequently, the *Scott Standard Postage Stamp Catalogue* does not list any Cuban stamps issued after that date.

However, for all practical purposes, the U.S. government will not seriously object if an American philatelist goes up to Canada, for example, and buys a few post-1962 stamps for his collection. The Federal authorities would object only if the collector started selling those stamps in relatively large quantities in order to make a profit.

Cuba's 1974 six-value "History of Baseball" set has attracted particularly favorable attention from hobbyists around the world. Full listings of all Cuban stamps can be found in the *Stanley Gibbons Stamp Catalogue* published in London, England.

"Sand Dunes" Issue (see opposite page)

U.S. Baseball Stamps

The United States has thus far issued six baseball stamps: (1) the 1939 3¢ (Scott #855) marking the centennial of baseball; (2) the 1969 6¢ (Scott #1381) commemorating the centennial of professional baseball; (3) the 1982 20¢ Jackie Robinson "Black Heritage" stamp (Scott #2016); (4) the 1983 20¢ Babe Ruth portrait (#2046); (5) the 1984 20¢ Roberto Clemente–Puerto Rican flag (Scott #2097); (6) the 1989 25¢ Lou Gehrig portrait (Scott #2417).

In our section on philatelic covers we see how collectors use these stamps in connection with commemorative cachets.

We might also consider the 1969 6¢ Grandma Moses "American Folklore" series specimen as a "quasi-baseball" stamp (Scott #1370). The stamp, based on Ms. Moses' painting "July Fourth," has a central vignette depicting a pick-up baseball game. Some sports philately enthusiasts omit this Grandma Moses issue because it wasn't turned out as a stamp specifically honoring baseball. Nevertheless, the ball game is a dominant feature in the painting.

The 1984 20¢ Jim Thorpe portrait stamp (Scott #2089) is another borderline U.S. baseball issue. Thorpe, generally considered to be "the greatest all-around athlete of all time," played major league baseball for six seasons (mostly with the New York Giants), but he is much better known for his prowess on the football field. On the stamp he is seen wearing his football togs.

(Opposite page) Ras al Khaima, one of the seven Arab Trucial States, issued a set of eight postage stamps in 1971 commemorating "Baseball Friendship" between the U.S. and Japan. A famous American ballplayer is portrayed with a Japanese star on each of the stamps. Seen are: 10d, Babe Ruth and Sadaharu Oh; 25d, Joe DiMaggio and Shigeo Nagashima; 30d, Stan Musial and Masaichi Kaneda; 50d, Ted Williams and Minoru Murayama; 70d, Willie Mays and Futashi Nakonishi; 80d, Roy Campanella and Katsuya Nomura; 1r, Ty Cobb and Tetsuharu Kawakami; and 1.50r, Lou Gehrig and Eiji Sawamura.

"Sand Dune" Issues

The United Arab Emirates (specifically, Ajman, Manama, Ras Al Khaima) have issued a profusion of baseball stamps, though little or no diamond game activity takes place in this Middle East region. Despite this, American collectors in particular favor these issues because of their excellent portraits of Hall of Fame ballplayers, including Honus Wagner, Joe DiMaggio, Ty Cobb, Stan Musial, Babe Ruth, George Sisler, Willie Mays, Reggie Jackson, Steve Carlton, and Ted Williams.

United Arab Emirates baseball issues of the late 1960s–early 1970s have appreciated tremendously in value in recent years and are becoming more and more difficult to find anywhere.

A wide array of baseball stamps has poured forth from countries of Latin America and the Caribbean, especially from locales like the Dominican Republic where baseball for all intents and purposes is the national game.

Baseball is played in the Dominican Republic the year round because of the favorable climate—and because legions of youngsters believe that by becoming professionals on the diamond they can break out of the proverbial "ghetto." Dozens of major leaguers, particularly middle infielders, have hailed from a single Dominican Republic city, San Pedro de Macoris, a sugar mill center, lying on the Caribbean some 35 miles east of Santo Domingo, the capital. The youngsters of San Pedro de Macoris and environs idolize major league ballplayers and wish to emulate them.

In recent years, a number of Caribbean countries, especially Grenada and St. Vincent, have gone in for turning out long sets of baseball stamps (totalling several hundred varieties) portraying diamond stars of the past and present. While these issues have remained highly popular among collectors, most astute observers of the philatelic field believe that the market may eventually become "saturated" if these stamps keep pouring forth in an unabated fashion.

As a footnote, we might add that Carl Yastrzemski, Hall of Fame Boston Red Sox slugger, wasn't thrilled with the 1989 St. Vincent $2 stamp carrying his portrait. Carl's name was badly

"SPOOK" JACOBS 2nd base KANSAS CITY ATHLETICS

Forrest Vandergrift "Spook" Jacobs, who played professional base-ball for 15 years, including three seasons in the big leagues (in 1954–56; with the Philadelphia and Kansas City Athletics, as well as with the Pittsburgh Pirates), now owns what is generally considered to be the finest private collection of baseball stamps in the world.

misspelled. We recall that when the American League presented him with a special trophy marking his selection as the circuit's Most Valuable Player for 1967, Yastrzemski immediately returned the trophy because his last name was butchered on the inscription line.

In regard to Asia, baseball is played widely and on a highly spirited basis in four countries in particular: the Republic of China (Taiwan), Japan (see separate chapter on Japan), Korea and the Philippines—and all four of these nations have produced numerous baseball stamps. Most of Taiwan's baseball issues deal with that country's remarkable run of victories in the "Little League World Series," played every August in Williamsport, Pa.

Taiwan has commemorated most of its Little League World Series championships with special stamps issued within a few weeks after the close of competition. For the most part these stamps have consisted of various inscription overprints on regular issues.

Cacheted Philatelic Baseball Covers

This is one of the most popular and widely collected segments in the entire baseball memorabilia field. Cacheted baseball covers have been produced by so many different philatelic societies and commercial organizations that it's almost literally impossible to catalogue them all. Certainly, there are a number of excellent references in the field with one of the best being *Baseball ... Stamps ... Autographs* by Elten F. Schiller, originally published in 1982, and recently updated and revised. Schiller recently retired as a vice president of the National League's San Diego Padres, but all inquiries regarding the ordering of *Baseball ... Stamps ... Autographs* can be directed to the San Diego Padres at P.O. Box 2000, San Diego, Calif. 92120.

In his book, Schiller also gives a listing of all world baseball stamps issued from 1934 through the 1980s. The first postage stamp dealing with baseball was turned out by the Philippine Islands on April 14, 1934, as part of a three-value set publicizing the "Tenth Far Eastern Championship Games." The 2-centavos value shows a batter getting ready to swing at a pitch with a catcher behind him.

Schiller and other experts in this collecting area emphasize that covers autographed by ballplayers are premium items. For example, he has a cover franked with the U.S. 6-cent baseball stamp postmarked at Cincinnati, Ohio, on Sept. 24, 1969 during first day ceremonies. The stamp commemorates the centennial of professional baseball (baseball's first professional team, the Cincinnati Red Stockings, began play in 1869), with a cachet featuring a portrait of Babe Ruth.

Schiller managed to get two players to sign this cover: Hank Aaron, who broke Ruth's all-time major league home run record of 714 (Aaron wound up with 755 round-trippers), and Roger Maris, who surpassed Ruth's one season record of 60 homers (Maris belted 61 in 1961). And, as Hank Aaron once said, "That Babe Ruth really gave us some gargantuan records to shoot at."

Ranked as the first authentic baseball cards issued in the U.S. these Adrian C. "Cap" Anson, John Clarkson and Mike "King" Kelly cards are from Allen & Ginter's 1887 "Champions of Sport" series. All three players have been elected into baseball's Hall of Fame. Only 10 of 50 Allen & Ginter "Champions of Sport" cards, in mint condition, sold for $8,500 (a record for the set) at an August 1990 Harrisburg, Pa., sports memorabilia auction.
(Photos, courtesy David Birmingham, Middletown, Pa.)

A

This cover, one of a 500 limited edition, commemorates the "shot heard round the world," the 35th anniversary of Bobby Thomson's dramatic homer with two outs in the ninth that carried the New York Giants to the 1951 pennant over the Brooklyn Dodgers.

This cover marks the 50th anniversary of the first televised base-ball game. It is signed by Walter Lanier "Red" Barber, who, from his "catbird seat," handled the telecast of the first game of a double-header between the Cincinnati Reds and Brooklyn Dodgers at Ebbets Field on August 26, 1939. Red described the action while sitting among the fans in the upper deck. With no tele-prompter to guide him, he ad-libbed commercials for Wheaties, Mobil Oil and Ivory Soap. After the game (won by Cincinnati 5-2), Barber conducted the first post-game TV interviews—with Dodger first baseman Dolph Camilli, and Leo Durocher and Bill McKechnie, managers of the Dodgers and Reds, respectively. The second game, won by Brooklyn 6-1, was not televised.

B

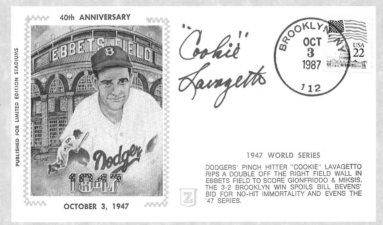

40th ANNIVERSARY

EBBETS FIELD

Dodger

1947

OCTOBER 3, 1947

"Cookie" Lavagetto

BROOKLYN N.Y.
OCT
3
1987
J 12

USA
22

1947 WORLD SERIES

DODGERS' PINCH HITTER "COOKIE" LAVAGETTO
RIPS A DOUBLE OFF THE RIGHT FIELD WALL IN
EBBETS FIELD TO SCORE GIONFRIDDO & MIKSIS.
THE 3-2 BROOKLYN WIN SPOILS BILL BEVENS'
BID FOR NO-HIT IMMORTALITY AND EVENS THE
'47 SERIES.

Harold "Cookie" Lavagetto, whose pinch-hit double in the 9th inning of the 4th game of the 1947 World Series spoiled Bill Bevens' bid for a no-hitter, signed this cover commemorating the 40th anniversary of one of the "Great Moments" in baseball history. The cover was postmarked at Brooklyn on Oct. 3, 1987.

Nicaragua's multi-colored 1972 souvenir sheet of four values publicizes the 20th International Baseball Championships held at Managua, the capital, from Nov. 15th to Dec. 5th of that year. A total of 23 countries participated in the competition.

ALEMANIA
ARUBA
AFRICA DEL SUR
BRASIL
COSTA RICA
CANADA

NICARAGUA AMIGA '72
15c AEREO
XX CAMPEONATO MUNDIAL DE BEISBOL AFICIONADO

CUBA
COLOMBIA
COREA DEL SUR
EL SALVADOR
ESTADOS UNIDOS
DE AMERICA

NICARAGUA AMIGA '72
20c AEREO
XX CAMPEONATO MUNDIAL DE BEISBOL AFICIONADO

XX
CAMPEONATO
MUNDIAL
DE BEISBOL
AFICIONADO
NOV. 15 DIC. 5, 1972
MANAGUA D. N.
NICARAGUA, C. A.

NICARAGUA AMIGA '72
40c AEREO
XX CAMPEONATO MUNDIAL DE BEISBOL AFICIONADO

GUATEMALA
HONDURAS
HOLANDA
ITALIA
JAPON
MEXICO

NICARAGUA AMIGA '72
10c AEREO
XX CAMPEONATO MUNDIAL DE BEISBOL AFICIONADO

NICARAGUA
PERU
PUERTO RICO
PANAMA
REP. DOMINICANA
VENEZUELA

C

Major League Baseball in Stamps

Under license from Major League Baseball, Grenada in 1988 issued nine miniature sheets portraying a total of 81 major league stars, past and present. Later on, MLB informed the government of Grenada that all Pete Rose portrait stamps must be withdrawn from sale.

D

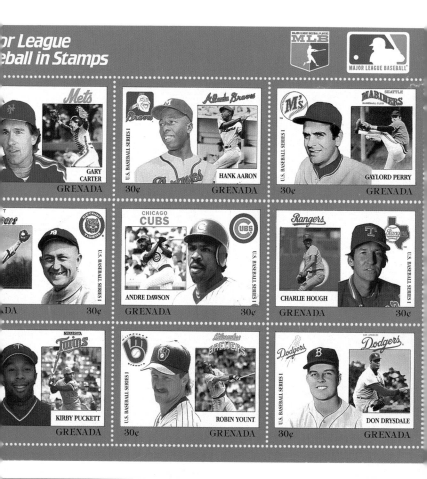

These sheets of Grenada stamps are selling for $35–40 per set of 9.

E

More than 50 countries around the world, including the United States, have collectively issued more than 1,000 baseball stamps. Baseball is now played in virtually every corner of the earth, including in the faraway Solomon Islands.

F

The Dominican Republic has issued numerous stamps depicting all phases of baseball since this Caribbean nation is a hotbed of diamond game activity. And, yes, baseball is played in Liberia.

Carl Yastrzemski wasn't too happy when he learned that his name was misspelled on a St. Vincent portrait stamp, but at least the printers didn't muff the spelling of Schoendienst.

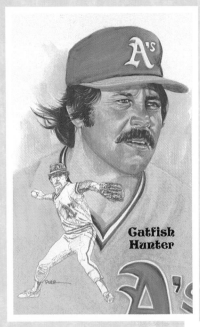

Catfish
Hunter

Dick Perez, who, as the Hall's official artist, has drawn portraits of all 204 HOF members, painted these portraits of Bobby Doerr (1986 inductee) and Jim "Catfish" Hunter (1987 inductee) from the "Post Card" series. The entire set of 206 cards is available from the Hall of Fame Gift Shop in Cooperstown. Dick Perez is generally regarded as baseball's most talented artist.

Jim "Catfish" Hunter, former Oakland A's star righthander, in 1975 became the first free agent to be signed by George Steinbrenner, flamboyant New York Yankees owner.

Ted Williams often said that Bobby Doerr, Boston Red Sox second baseman and longtime teammate, was the "smoothest" infielder he ever saw. Doerr was also a powerful righthanded slugger who could literally write his name on Fenway Park's left field wall, the "Green Monster."

Bobby
Doerr

H

Schiller illustrates many cacheted covers bearing the June 12, 1939 U.S. 3-cent issue marking the centennial of baseball. (The stamp features a vignette of a sandlot ball game.) One of the covers, bearing a cachet featuring the stylized figure of a powerful batter, is autographed by the ten players who were inducted into the Hall of Fame inaugural ceremonies on June 12, 1939: Walter Johnson, Grover Cleveland Alexander, Babe Ruth, Ty Cobb, Honus Wagner, Tris Speaker, George Sisler, Eddie Collins, Nap Lajoie and Cy Young. An autographed cover of this type is worth several thousands of dollars.

Elten Schiller also illustrates and describes several of the many cacheted covers produced by the Rockford, Illinois, Philatelic Society. Among them is a specimen postmarked at Rockford on March 24, 1979. The cover publicizes the Rockford Philatelic group's annual convention and exhibition, while the cachet consists of portraits of two Hall of Fame ballplayers who came to the convention as special guests, Stan Musial and Lou Boudreau. The cover, which also commemorates the 40th anniversary of the founding of the Hall of Fame at Cooperstown, is a classic item when it bears the Musial and Boudreau signatures.

Brooklyn Dodgers Covers

Scott Forst of Huntington Station, Long Island, New York, who founded a memorabilia company called Limited Edition Stadiums more than a decade ago, specializes in producing covers with Brooklyn Dodgers themes. The Dodgers, who were based in Brooklyn for 68 consecutive seasons, from 1890 through 1957, moved to Los Angeles in 1958. Brooklyn baseball fans have never forgiven Dodger owner Walter O'Malley for leaving "Flatbush."

One of Forst's many covers recalling the great days of the Dodgers in Brooklyn, is a specimen postmarked at Brooklyn on Oct. 2, 1988, and franked with two stamps: the 20-cent Jackie Robinson stamp, and a 5-cent US flag issue. (The flag stamp had to be added since the first class rate was 25 cents.) The cover marks the 35th anniversary of Carl Erskine's 14-strikeout performance in the World Series against the New York Yankees on Oct. 2, 1953 at Brooklyn's Ebbets Field. Erskine, the Dodgers' star righthander of the time, bested the Yankees 3–2 in that historic game as he went the distance—and at that point in baseball history no one had struck out more batters in a World Series game than had Erskine. (Bob Gibson of the St. Louis Cardinals broke Erskine's record when on Oct. 2, 1968 he struck out 17 Detroit Tigers in a route-going 4–0 victory in the first game of the '68 World Series, played at St. Louis.)

The Dodgers lost that '53 World Series to the Yankees 4 games to 2, but Erskine's performance was one of the most brilliant in World Series annals.

The Forst cover features a colored cachet of Erskine pitching against the background of Brooklyn's Ebbets Field, and a limited number of those covers are inscribed with Erskine's signature, making them premium memorabilia items.

Many of Forst's covers deal with great moments from the 1955 World Series when the Dodgers edged out the Yankees 4 games to 3 in one of the most dramatic "Fall Classics" ever played.

As Scott Forst said recently: "The Dodgers may have moved out of Brooklyn a generation ago, but the glory lives on forever!"

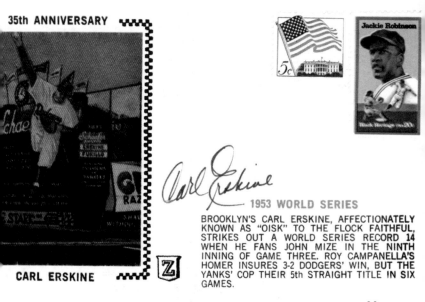

35th ANNIVERSARY

CARL ERSKINE

1953 WORLD SERIES

BROOKLYN'S CARL ERSKINE, AFFECTIONATELY KNOWN AS "OISK" TO THE FLOCK FAITHFUL, STRIKES OUT A WORLD SERIES RECORD 14 WHEN HE FANS JOHN MIZE IN THE NINTH INNING OF GAME THREE. ROY CAMPANELLA'S HOMER INSURES 3-2 DODGERS' WIN, BUT THE YANKS' COP THEIR 5th STRAIGHT TITLE IN SIX GAMES.

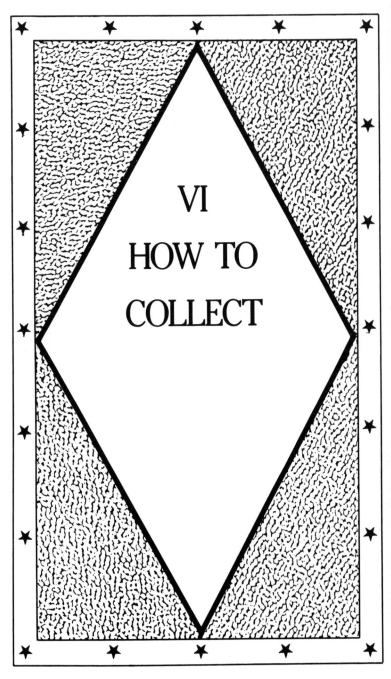

VI

HOW TO

COLLECT

Beware of Fake Cards and Fake Autographs!

"Anything of value has at one time or another been either counterfeited, faked or forged" goes the old maxim—and this same principle holds true for baseball memorabilia as well. For example, the famed Honus Wagner Sweet Caporal cigarette card of 1910 (valued at close to $150,000 for specimen in Mint condition) has been counterfeited numerous times, along with such other noted cards as the Mickey Mantle and Pete Rose "Rookie" cards of 1951 and 1963.

Jim Cobb (born 1921) the youngest son of the great Ty Cobb, told this writer that his father's signature has been faked continuously over a period of many years. Jim Cobb said:

"During the Hall of Fame Induction Ceremonies Week-End during the first week of August in 1990, I walked into a Cooperstown memorabilia shop and noticed that three of my father's supposed autographs were being offered for sale—and at hundreds of dollars each. Each of the 'autographs' was clearly a forgery and I told the dealer as much, who promised to withdraw them from sale. Maybe the dealer knew the signatures were fakes, maybe he didn't, but I told him plainly enough that I can readily tell the difference between a true Ty Cobb autograph and a forgery."

The moral of this tale is that any baseball memorabilia collector should trade only with established dealers.

Collectors should be wary of caps and jerseys that have been manufactured in huge wholesale lots and then deceptively offered as authentic big league baseball garb. Genuine Brooklyn Dodgers caps with the "B" logo manufactured prior to 1957, for example, are extremely valuable, but facsimiles have been produced by the thousands and possess little value.

If any dealer knowingly sells counterfeit merchandise, he would be liable for prosecution. In any event, the collector is entitled to a full refund if he can show that he purchased counterfeit, forged or fake material.

Barry Halper, Super Collector

"Go ahead, ring the doorbell," Barry Halper said as we approached the front door of his spacious and handsome northern New Jersey home. Upon touching the button, we didn't hear an ordinary buzz or chime . . . what we heard was a chimed rendition of "Take Me Out to the Ball Game."

And once passing through the door we spent several hours viewing what unquestionably ranks as the world's largest and finest privately held collection of baseball memorabilia. Barry Halper, for example, owns more than 900 uniform jerseys, or more than enough to outfit every player on the 26 teams now in the two major leagues.

Then he has more than 5,000 autographed baseballs, and over 1.2 million baseball cards. His array of all types of baseball collectibles literally boggles the imagination. The entire collection is insured for many millions of dollars.

The collection also includes over 1,000 baseball bats, from the earliest types used in the mid-19th century to contemporary models. Besides, Barry has at least 1,000 different examples of baseball sheet music, dozens of huge scrapbooks bulging with thousands of magazine and newspaper clippings covering the entire history of the diamond game, as well as dozens of other types of baseball memorabilia.

Just who is Barry Halper? And what are the forces that drove him to build this massive private baseball museum? Barry, born in 1939, is president of Halper Brothers, Inc., an Edison N.J.-based company specializing in the distribution of paper and packaging products and maintenance supplies. The firm, founded by his grandfather in 1910, maintains a delivery fleet of more than 70 trucks.

Barry's collecting interests go back to his elementary school days in the Newark, N.J. area where he lived within a 25-mile radius of the home stadiums of the New York Giants, Brooklyn

Barry Halper, part owner of the New York Yankees, has the world's largest private baseball memorabilia collection.

Dodgers, New York Yankees, Newark Bears and Jersey City Giants. He lived closest, however, to the International League Newark team. Halper would stop by the stadium on his way home from school, and his father would pick him up on his way home after work.

"I used to hang around and get autographs," explained Halper. "One day, Lou Novikoff of the Newark Bears told me, 'Come back tomorrow and I'll give you something to make you stop asking for autographs.' So I went back there the next day and he gave me his *uniform*. 'Now I'm free from your badgering for autographs,' he said."

As Halper grew, so too, did his enthusiasm for collecting. As for uniforms, his assemblage today is considered to be superior to the one held by the Baseball Hall of Fame Museum at Cooperstown, and it all started with Lou Novikoff's "contribution to the cause."

Barry Halper's amazing array of those 900-plus uniforms constitutes, perhaps, the most valuable section of his entire collection.

On our tour through this baseball fantasyland, he took hold of a remote control device, similar to a TV tuner, that caused a window-sized panel to slide away at a single touch. Inside, were all the uniforms fitted onto an enormous clothing rack such as used at dry-cleaning establishments. Halper can make the rack rotate and stop at whatever uniform he wants by simply pressing the complex control gadget.

"This is all computer-controlled," he chortled, almost gleefully. "Temperature and humidity controlled, too."

By scanning this multitude of uniforms one can see almost the entire span of professional baseball history coming to life. There are uniforms from baseball's rough-and-tumble days of the 1870s to 1890s, clear on through to the multicolored double-knit polyesters that players wear today. Among his latest acquisitions are two vintage Boston Red Stockings jerseys worn by star players more than a century ago.

There are seven Babe Ruth uniforms in the collection, including at least one type from every team that Ruth played for, or coached, on a professional basis—except for one, the Providence uniform of the International League team, where he pitched for only a couple of weeks in 1914.

Included are: a Ruth Baltimore International League uniform of 1914, a Boston Red Sox uniform, also of 1914, several New York Yankees uniforms with the famous No. 3, a Boston Bees (Braves) uniform of 1935, and one from the Brooklyn Dodgers—where the Babe coached briefly in 1938. (In the mid-30s, the Braves were temporarily known as the Bees.)

Halper is actively pursuing all possibilities in trying to acquire a 1914 Providence Babe Ruth jersey.

Since original Babe Ruth uniforms are extremely scarce and in such great demand by collectors, Halper value them conservatively at approximately $25,000 each.

Part of the DiMaggio Room in Barry Halper's collection.

He has placed one of Ruth's No. 3 Yankees uniforms on a life-size wax replica of the Bambino that he acquired for $900 from Madame Tussaud's Wax Museum in London. He learned that the wax figure was available because Tussaud's was updating the exhibition and had planned to place the Babe in storage.

Halper has several Lou Gehrig uniforms, including one that the fabled "Iron Horse" wore while he played for Columbia University in 1921–22.

Perhaps the most unusual of the Gehrig uniforms is the one worn while he was with Hartford in the Eastern League during the summer of 1921.

In order to protect his college eligibility, Gehrig played under his names of Henry Louis, without the Gehrig. The "Henry Louis" was sewn in small letters into the shirt and knickers as laundry identification marks.

Bats Galore

Barry Halper has so many bats that this part of his collection almost looks and smells like a lumber yard, or like Hillerich & Bradsby's warehouse in Louisville.

There are wooden bats from baseball's so-called "Stone Age" of the 19th century right down to the ones used in the 1980s.

Among the earliest historic specimens is a bat presented in 1870 to Cincinnati Red Stockings' manager Harry Wright, to commemorate the team's 100 consecutive victories. The inscription on the bat notes this historic feat. The Red Stockings won their last 8 games in 1868, all 69 in 1869 and their first 23 in 1870 to achieve that milestone. Actually, the streak ran to 130—believe it or not—before manager Wright's team finally lost to the Brooklyn Atlantics on June 14, 1870.

One of Halper's prized possessions from baseball's earliest days is the bat used by big Dan Brouthers, who won five big league batting championships from 1882 to 1892—with Buffalo, Boston and Brooklyn. Elected to the Hall of Fame in 1945 largely on the basis of his lifetime .342 batting average, Brouthers swung a long and heavy bat. He was a long ball hitter, but he settled mostly for doubles and triples, since it was so tough in those days to knock the "dead ball" for homers.

A Wee Willie Keeler model bat, recently obtained by Halper, is much smaller than the Brouthers type. Keeler, who "hit 'em where they ain't," went mostly for singles and won two batting crowns while with the Baltimore Orioles in 1897–98, finishing with lofty marks of .432 and .379, respectively.

"You can easily tell what kind of hitter a man is—or was—just by looking at his bat," Halper said.

Among the historic early 20th century bats in the collection is a "Shoeless" Joe Jackson big "Black Betsy," the type he used to compile a big league batting mark of .356 from 1908 to 1920. The bat, a long and stout one, is inscribed with Shoeless Joe's full signature. If a bat like this were to come up at public auction, it would draw a winning bid well up into the thousands of dollars.

The heaviest of all game-used bats in Halper's collection is the 48-ounce bludgeon of Edd Roush, who won two National League batting titles while with Cincinnati in 1917 (.341) and 1919 (.321).

Roush himself once said, "My 48-ounce bat was the heaviest anyone ever used, I think. It was a shorter bat, with a big handle, and I tried to hit to all fields. Didn't swing my head off, just snapped at the ball."

Halper has several of Babe Ruth's bats. They're big too, weighing only a couple of ounces less than Roush's, but they're much longer and were designed for long-distance belting.

Perhaps the most unusual of all the bats Halper owns is the bottle-shaped type used by Heinie Groh, who played for 16 years in the National League (1912–27), mostly with New York and Cincinnati. The bat, made by Spalding, has a thin handle and a very thick barrel, making it possible for Groh to punch out singles. He batted .292 lifetime and was difficult to strike out, fanning only 345 times in 6,074 official at-bats.

Several years ago, Halper loaned the Heinie Groh bottle bat to Woody Allen who needed it for a prop in his movie "Zelig." Somehow during the shooting, this rare bat was broken. "I did my best to have it patched up, but it's lost a great deal of its value as a repaired bat," said Halper.

The Roger Connor Weathervane

Adorning the top of Halper's house is a weathervane constructed out of a couple of old baseball bats that once belonged to Hall-of-Famer Roger Connor. Connor, a hard-hitting National League first baseman from 1883 to 1897, mostly with New York and St. Louis, was the home run king of the dead-ball era. His 138 homers were the career record for major leaguers until surpassed by Babe Ruth in 1921.

A fan is said to have presented the weathervane to Connor in the early 1890s, and Connor proceeded to place it atop his house in Waterbury, Conn. Halper, who specializes in memorabilia related to Hall-of-Famers, had little Connor material, save for an autograph or two. Barry learned about the weathervane while reading Marty Appel's book, *The Hall of Fame Gallery*. In the chapter on Roger Connor, there was a picture of the Waterbury house topped by the baseball bat weathervane.

Believing that the weathervane would be an ideal addition to his collection, Barry called the Waterbury Chamber of Commerce to ask if the Connor house was still standing. Here's how Barry went on to relate the rest of the story:

"They told me the house was converted into a factory, and then I called the factory about the weathervane. The guy at the factory thought I was crazy, but conceded it was still up there on the roof. I told him I would not only pay for it, but that I'd also pay a couple of his workers to go up there and get it down."

That's how Barry Halper, the Super Collector operates . . . once he makes up his mind to get an unusual bit of memorabilia, he'll make an all-out effort and won't take "no" for an answer. He considers the Roger Connor weathervane one of his strongest links to baseball's "Stone Age."

Bresnahan's Shinguards

Among the vintage specimens of baseball equipment in Halper's collection is one of the first pairs of shinguards ever worn— Roger "Duke" Bresnahan's. The Hall-of-Fame catcher, who spent most of his big league playing days with the New York Giants and St. Louis Cardinals, while with the Giants in 1907, introduced shinguards. Everybody laughed at him in 1907, but today no catcher or plate umpire would think of going into a game without them.

The Bresnahan shinguards Halper has in his den are obviously the same basic type as those being used by ballplayers today. Bresnahan was also the first to experiment with a batting helmet. After sustaining a severe beaning, he felt additional protection for the head was essential.

Casey Stengel's Yearbook

The variety of material acquired by Halper over the years staggers the imagination. He even has a copy of Casey Stengel's high school yearbook, a softcover volume published in 1909 from the graduating class of Centralia, Kansas High School. (Centralia is a small town in the northeastern part of the state.)

The yearbook tells us that Casey starred on the school's basketball team as well as on the baseball team. Where else would we see the future "Old Professor" dressed in a basketball uniform. An item like this would bring a substantial sum at a baseball memorabilia auction.

Baseball Music

In recent years Barry Halper has devoted a great deal of effort to building up the baseball music section of his collection—well over 1,000 examples of baseball sheet music and records.

"Music is an integral part of the game," emphasized Halper. "Many clubs hire professional organists—and even bands—to play at games, and I've been keenly interested in trying to come up with at least one copy of every bit of music ever written about the game."

If Barry Halper's collection of baseball sheet music isn't complete at this writing, it's very close to that goal. He has, for starters, a copy of the oldest known baseball song, a number published in 1858 called "The Baseball Polka," dedicated to the Niagara Baseball Club of Buffalo, N.Y. "The Baseball Polka" came out exactly 50 years before Jack Norworth published "Take Me Out to the Ball Game" in 1908, which has since become baseball's unofficial anthem. Norworth wrote the words, while his collaborator, Albert von Tilzer, composed the music. Halper has innumerable varieties of "Take Me Out to the Ball Game" sheet music published in 1908 and in subsequent years.

Halper recently acquired an unusual item—a Jack Norworth brand cigar box, with the songwriter's color photo featured on the cover.

"I paid $60 for this rare cigar box," Halper said, "but if the seller knew that Norworth wrote 'Take Me Out to the Ball Game,' I think he would have wanted more."

One of the most valuable specimens of baseball sheet music in Halper's collection is entitled "The National Game—Dedicated to Judge Kenesaw Mountain Landis," a march composed by John Philip Sousa in the early 1920s. Sousa, "The March King," also composed such classics as "The Stars and Stripes Forever" and "Semper Fidelis."

Halper idolized Joe DiMaggio as a ballplayer since early boyhood and has invited the "Yankee Clipper" to inspect his private museum several times. Several years ago Halper had a special wooden and glass exhibit case constructed to hold exactly 56 official American League baseballs, or one for each game of Joe DiMaggio's heralded 56-game hitting streak achieved during the 1941 season. Naturally, every one of the baseballs has DiMaggio's autograph inscribed on it.

Halper has been extremely generous in allowing legions of writers and baseball historians to visit and utilize his collection for research purposes. And in order to allow the general public to get at least a glimpse of the baseball museum, he made a half-hour video in 1989 featuring the most interesting and valuable items. Halper himself narrates the video with the assistance of the late Billy Martin, ex-manager of the New York Yankees, etc.

Halper donated the proceeds from the video (which became a nationwide best-seller) to the burn unit at St. Barnabas Hospital in Livingston, New Jersey.

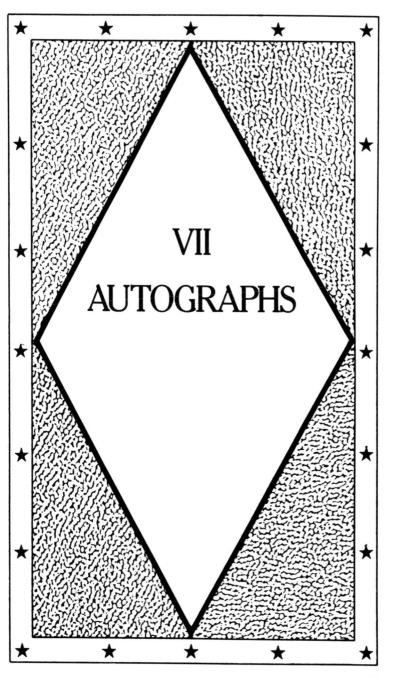

VII

AUTOGRAPHS

From Free Autographs
To Charging $30 a Line

Back in 1947, Greenberg: Publisher in New York City released Joe DiMaggio's autobiography *Lucky To Be A Yankee* and scheduled an autograph party for "Joltin' Joe" at Bamberger's Department Store in Newark.

At the scheduled hour for the signing session, the line of fans, mostly youngsters, waiting to get a glimpse of DiMag, stretched through the store and around the block . . . and a table next to Joe was stacked high with copies of his $2.50 paperback book. One of the youngsters near the head of the line, a boy of about 11 or 12, didn't have the money to buy a book but he had a little square piece of paper to give DiMaggio. The Yankee Clipper unhesitatingly signed it.

Word then spread like wildfire that Joe D was signing autographs gratis—and at the end of the session that ran for nearly two hours the Yankees centerfielder had graciously signed hundreds of autographs, mostly on odd scraps of paper that the kids hustled together.

A representative from the publishers observed at the time: "We wound up selling at best 5 or 6 copies of DiMaggio's book . . . and the fans went home happy, but from a pure business point of view the autograph session was a flop."

Would an episode like this take place today? Hardly likely. Baseball stars of past and present like to charge for their autographs, and certainly none of them would think of giving autographs away at book-signing sessions.

For example, Carl Yastrzemski, Boston Red Sox outfield star for 23 years (1961–83) and a 1989 Hall of Fame inductee, came out in the spring of 1990 with his autobiography titled *Yaz: Baseball, the Wall and Me*. The huge Barnes & Noble bookstore, which occupies a good part of a block on Fifth Avenue in midtown Manhattan, lined up Yastrzemski for what was supposed to be an hour-long signing session on a weekday afternoon. The session stretched to nearly two hours as Yaz wound up signing more than 600 copies of his tome, a store record for the sale of any book in one day.

And not a single autograph was given away—anyone who wanted Yaz' signature had to plunk down $18.50 for the book before Carl would give any examples of his penmanship. And this happened in New York, Home of the Yankees, arch-rivals of the Red Sox. In Boston, Yastrzemski went on to sign carloads of his autobio at a series of bookstore appearances.

Collecting Autographs by Topic

Dedicated autograph hunters like to collect star signatures by topic. For example, getting all the living "500 Home Run Hitters" to sign the same baseball presents a real challenge.

Thus, in 1989 enterprising card show promoters, in order to accommodate topical collectors, staged an extravaganza at one of the Atlantic City, N.J., casinos where all living 500-homer hitters were present to sign everything from baseballs, to bats, uniform jerseys, etc. (for fat fees, of course).

Present were Ernie Banks, Eddie Mathews, Willie McCovey, Ted Williams, Mickey Mantle, Mike Schmidt, Reggie Jackson, Harmon Killebrew, Frank Robinson, Willie Mays and Hank Aaron— the 11 living 500-homer belting sluggers. Thousands of autograph-hungry fans jammed their way into one of the casino's spacious ballrooms to collect signatures from this stellar group.

Show promoters also work to gather together all living pitchers with 300 or more major-league victories to their credit. This group includes Tom Seaver, Don Sutton, Gaylord Perry, Early Wynn, Phil Niekro, Warren Spahn and Steve Carlton.

Steve Carlton, who made it a point of never talking to reporters for the last decade or so of his active career (because he became turned off by reports when one of them supposedly "misquoted" him), enjoys attending card shows featuring the "300 victory club." And when he's scribbling away at one of the autograph tables he's affable and charming—he becomes a veritable babbling brook when fans want to speak with him.

The Card Show Phenomenon

Demand for autographs from the diamond stars is so great that the "Card Show" phenomenon really began taking off in about 1980. Simply defined, a Card Show is a baseball memorabilia convention (or "mini-convention") that may draw anywhere from 10 to more than 500 dealers who offer their wares at tables and booths.

"Card" is the key word since the baseball card remains as the most widely popular of any type of baseball collectible. At a Card Show, however, various dealers may offer many hundreds of different types of items, ranging from baseball books, to vintage jerseys to razor blades once used (or supposedly used) by Babe Ruth.

Players, both current and retired, are almost invariably invited to these shows as "Drawing Cards." For example, if a show promoter advertises that Joe DiMaggio or Tom Seaver will be appearing at one of his events for an autograph session, the building may not be big enough to hold the surging crowds.

When Joe D began appearing at these shows in the early 1980s, his fee per autograph began at something like $6 to $8, but at those prices there seemed to be no end to the lines of fans waiting to lay down their money for an intimate moment with a man generally labeled as "The Greatest Living Ex-Ballplayer."

Toward the mid-to-late 1980s, DiMag raised his fee to $15 per signature. This decision caused numerous complaints from baseball addicts around the country who now felt that DiMaggio was charging a bit much for his signature. In fact, the term "Yankee Clipper" started to be used in derision. What was Joe D's answer to all this criticism? Why, he simply raised the price to $18 and the lines forming at his autograph sessions were just as long as ever!

Remember, inflationary pressures always seem to affect the baseball memorabilia mania that continues into the 1990s. DiMaggio's fees kept in step with those pressures. At this moment his fee stands at a cool $30 per signature. And even at the age of 76, the old Yankee Clipper maintains a bold and strong writing style. He signs his name in the same way he played the game.

Word gets around as to signing pay scales for baseball stars on the Card Show circuit, with Joe DiMaggio's fees acting as a kind of barometer for the entire "autograph industry." Other renowned Hall of Famers, like Ted Williams and Mickey Mantle, have said in effect: "If DiMaggio gets $30 for an autograph, then I've got to get 30 bucks also."

And fans—as fanatical as they are about rubbing elbows with the greats of the game—are more than willing to pay those fees. Moreover, collectors are more than willing to spend an hour or two waiting in line before they put down their $30 on the table for a superstar autograph. In some cases, a collector may want as many as 10 DiMaggio or Williams autographs at a time—and you can multiply $30 times 10 for yourself. Heavy money changes hands at those autograph sessions.

Willie Mays who has become a semi-regular on the Card Show circuit, charges by the hour, as do a number of other baseball notables. Through 1989, Willie's rate was a flat $4,000 per hour, plus expenses, and he'd have to be guaranteed by the show's sponsors at least three hours for a session. In this case, show promoters have to set a per autograph price high enough to cover a fat hourly rate of that magnitude. Then expenses may run to at least a couple of thousand bucks if Willie has to fly in to a New York show from California.

As one New York promoter told us: "Early in 1990, Willie Mays raised his hourly rate to $5,000 per hour and there are guys running Card Shows willing to lay out that kind of money because the 'Say Hey' kid brings in the crowds and virtually guarantees the success of any type of event. Dealers have to pay fees for their tables and booths, of course, and once a fan has his Mays autograph he may well wander over to the bourse area and spend some more money."

Willie Mays remains as one of the giants on the Card Show circuit despite the fact that he acts like the quintessential grouch at many of them, refusing for example, to look up at the fans as he signs, or not paying attention to a collector who wants a ball, a poster, photograph, or whatever, to be signed in a certain place. One fan told us after an encounter with Willie at a Card Show: "Willie the Wonder is an independent cuss. Just let him sign anywhere, anywhere he wants. If you tell·him to sign a poster on the *top*, he may sign it on the *bottom*. Just hand him your bit of memorabilia and take your chances. Sometimes he signs so fast his signature is not even legible, but we have to let Willie be Willie."

Almost all the big stars on the Circuit have their own peculiar idiosyncrasies. Mickey Mantle, for example, always has a printed sign on his table reading, "Mr. Mantle does not sign bats."

It seems that at one show in particular, a couple of youngsters aiming to get their bats signed by Mickey got into a dispute as to their place in line. In the resultant fight, they used their bats, when they ran out of words. From that point on, Mantle wanted no one in line to have a bat in his hands, deeming they could be used as lethal weapons.

At a July 1988 Card Show in Cincinnati, held at the time of the major league All-Star Game there, Mickey Mantle attracted legions of fans to his autograph table. One of the several hundreds of persons standing in line was a veteran Cincinnati baseball writer who spent more than an hour waiting for Mantle to sign his baseball for $15 (Mickey's going rate at the time). Another baseball writer asked him why he waited in line to spend the $15.

The answer was: "That was my moment with the Mick. It was well worth the 15 bucks because Mickey recognized me, smiled and even shook my hand."

Sometimes card show promoters lay out substantial sums of money to get oldtime players out to an event. The promoter who wants to make sure his star of yesteryear reaches the show as scheduled often sends out enough money for travel expenses—it may be the price of an air ticket from California to New York, and that's not cheap.

> BULLETIN!
> While Willie Mays' $5,000 per hour fee for appearing at autograph shows might seem to be an extraordinarily big number, the "Say Hey" kid has recently been eclipsed in the Card Show "Dollar Derby." Jose Canseco, the Oakland Athletics home run slugger, demands $50,000 per card show appearance!

On one occasion, an ex-diamond star who was in his early 80s flew into New York from a distant town and got to the show on time. But after signing autographs for a couple of hours he fainted, almost dead away. The show promoter promptly hustled him off to a back room, gave him smelling salts and led him back to the autograph table so he could fulfill the terms of his contract.

Naturally, it would have been better to have excused the old-timer for the day, but business is business.

A fan from Long Island, obviously in a philosophical mood, set down his views on the topic at a bit more length. He wrote: "In Utopia, athletes do not get paid for spending their off days signing thousands of autographs, copies of the *New York Times* are free, and hospitals don't charge for their services. In the United States, commodities in demand are sold for profit, and prices are controlled by supply and demand. If athletes did not get paid for signing thousands of autographs, they wouldn't do the shows and prices would be much higher because of the lower supply. So, what's all the fuss about? The shows are handled in relative good taste, and the fans couldn't be happier."

Autographed Baseballs

A baseball inscribed with the Hall of Fame logo was taken into space aboard the space shuttle "Atlantis," December 2–6, 1988, and signed by the five astronauts who made the flight: Robert "Hoot" Gibson, Guy Gardner, Mike Mullane, Bill Shepherd and Jerry Ross.

An official National League ball signed in mid-season 1989 by Ken Griffey, Sr. (Cincinnati Reds) and Ken Griffey, Jr. (Seattle Mariners), the first father-son combination to play in the major leagues at the same time. The ball was given to the HOF by a Mariners executive.

A 1985 Wisconsin yellow metal automobile license plate inscribed "America's Dairyland/BAG 270/Wisconsin 85." The "BAG" are the initials of the famous pitcher, Burleigh Arland Grimes, with the "270" representing the old spitballer's major league victories. Grimes went 270–212 in a 19-year major league career (1916–34).

Speaking of automobile licenses, the HOF Museum also has Cy Young's 1954 Ohio plate which is inscribed "511-CY." The 511 pertains to Young's major league record of 511 victories.

"We've noticed that serious memorabilia collectors visit the museum in order to get ideas as to how they can mount their own materials for display," said Peter Clark. "They also gain insights from us as to how they can build and organize their own collections."

The Hall of Fame Museum in Cooperstown contains every type of baseball memorabilia imaginable—from baseball cards by the bushel, to autographed baseballs by the thousands, to bats, gloves, uniforms, photo files, books, films, audio cassettes, phonograph records, paintings, etc.

Nevertheless, the prime exhibit at the Hall of Fame Museum remains that tattered and battered old "Abner Doubleday Baseball" supposedly used in the first ball game ever played in 1839, according to legend. The ball is prominently displayed in a specially constructed exhibit case on the museum's main floor where it has been viewed by several million baseball aficionados over the past 50-odd years.

Should Ballplayers Accept Payment for Autographs?

"When I sign a baseball the value of that ball increases. . . . and chances are the person who owns the item is going to sell it for a profit at some future date. Then why shouldn't I collect a fee for placing my signature on the ball and sharing in the profit?" So said Pete Rose, and there are legions of players and ex-players who agree with him on this point.

Nevertheless, legions of fans strenuously object to ballplayers signing autographs for money and they constantly write to the "Letters" sections of both the general and sporting press to that effect. As one fan from Staten Island said in a letter to *The New York Times* in the spring of 1990:

"Athletes should not accept money for autographs. My feeling is that they owe it to their fans. The people are responsible for their success, popularity and their great salaries. They are given the privilege to do what they love to do and get paid for it."

The *Times*, which conducted a fan's "Symposium" an autograph fees for athletes in that particular edition, ran a variety of other letters on the subject, with a fan from New York City observing:

"It's a free country. Why shouldn't athletes accept money for autographs? A better question, but one I can't answer: Why would a sane person pay for one?"

A reader from Brooklyn wrote in part: "I don't resent the old-time retired ballplayers who sign for cash. Most of them could use additional income and are willing to chat at length about the old days. That's what baseball is all about."

Autograph Mania in Cooperstown At the Hall of Fame

Autographs of Hall of Fame ballplayers carry premium values, of course, and wherever HOFers congregate autograph hounds are sure to follow. The year's largest gathering of Hall of Famers occurs every midsummer when Induction ceremonies for new HOF enshrinees take place at Cooperstown, that small picturesque upstate New York village lying on the shores of shimmering Lake Otsego.

All living Hall of Famers are invited (all expenses paid) to witness the Induction of the newest member of that very exclusive group of athletes . . . and ordinarily about 25 to 30 HOFers accept the invitation.

The late Hank Greenberg stopped attending the annual ceremonies in the 1960s because he was constantly besieged for autographs—everywhere from the grand old Hotel Otesaga, official hostelry for the distinguished visitors, to Doubleday Field (where a major league exhibition game is played on the day following the Inductions), and all around town.

Said Greenberg: "People used to ask me to sign dozens of baseballs at a time. . . . they followed me everywhere, and I couldn't help but being annoyed."

Sandy Koufax, as well as a number of other Hall of Famers, stopped going to Cooperstown for the same reason.

One time in the early 1970s, Joe DiMaggio hustled himself away from the Otesaga lobby, which was filled with autograph seekers, and repaired to the privacy of his second floor room. Later that evening, DiMag heard a tap-tap-tapping on his window. Who was it?. . . . why, it was an enterprising autograph seeker who somehow found out Joe D's room number, climbed up the fire escape, and made his autograph request. The startled DiMaggio immediately called hotel security and the autograph hound spent the night in the Cooperstown jail. The charge was "aggravated harassment," or something of that nature.

Nowadays, the Otesaga lobby is patrolled by hotel security,

and no one is allowed to enter at HOF Induction Ceremony time except registered guests.

Through most of the 1980s, Hall of Fame officials tried to placate the autograph hunters by staging "official" signing sessions on the spacious grounds of the Otesaga hotel where the HOFers would sit at long tables and sign one autograph per fan. At least one of these "official" sessions would be designated for youngsters 15 and under. In order for reasonable order to be maintained, each fan was given a number by an HOF staffer insuring his proper place in line.

This system seemed to work fairly well for a number of years . . . unfortunately, too many fans became unruly and made demands to get multiple autographs from the HOFers. This caused officials of the Baseball Museum to cancel the signature sessions entirely.

Moreover, professional dealers hired youngsters to get autographs for them at the "15 and under" sessions, and the numbers printed on cards giving fans their places in line were bought and sold like commodities.

"For multiple reasons we had to cross these autograph sessions off our calendar," commented one HOF executive.

The Mania Grows

If a prominent ballplayer of the past or present is spotted in public today, he'll generally be mobbed for his autograph because "Autograph Mania" has now reached almost epidemic proportions. Hall of Fame members in particular are subject to being hotly pursued by "Big Name Hunters."

Even elderly Hall of Famers who have a difficult time getting around these days are not exempt—they are being besieged for their signatures via the mail route.

Albert Benjamin "Happy" Chandler, baseball commissioner from 1945–51 (elected to the HOF as an executive), appeared on the card show circuit as a semi-regular until he was almost 90. But even after doctors ordered him to stop traveling, he continued signing everything from baseballs, to photos, and yearbooks, etc., by the thousands out of his Kentucky home.

Chandler, however, was a businessman and he didn't sign for free. (Chandler, a former Kentucky governor and U.S. senator, managed to build up a tidy fortune through his myriad of business contacts). His autographing at home was under the auspices of a New York-based organization that runs card shows and organizes "private signings." Thus, Chandler was able to net $5 or $6 per autograph. Even as he passed the age of 92, Happy Chandler kept hammering out his autograph as the dollars continued to roll in.

Hall of Fame signatures constitute the creme de la creme in the baseball memorabilia field and Happy Chandler, as an authentic Hall of Famer, was more than happy to be caught up in the web of the autograph craze.

Edd J. Roush, a 1917 and 1919 National League batting champion and a 1962 Hall of Fame inductee, lived on to the ripe old age of 93 (he died in 1986), Roush spent most of the last two or three years of his life scribbling his signature for collectors who sought him out through the mails—or even knocked on the door of his Indiana home. And Roush, a sharp businessman in the tradition of A. B. Chandler, hardly ever signed for free.

Those intrepid collectors specializing in HOF material, wanted to make sure they got hold of a good Roush signature before old Edd J. passed into the Great Beyond.

Other elderly Hall of Famers who have engaged in "private signings" organized by various card show operators include Bill Dickey, Rick Ferrell, Johnny Mize, Early Wynn, Ralph Kiner, Charlie Gehringer, Al Lopez, Steve Carlton and Robin Roberts.

Back when this writer worked for and with the Cleveland Indians from the late 1940s through the early 1950s, we constantly ran into great old ballplayers—including an array of Hall of Famers—who constantly paraded in and out of old League Park and Cleveland Stadium.

There was old third baseman Bill Bradley, then past 70 but still working as a Cleveland Indians scout who started his major league career in 1899 and whose play with the Indians from 1901 (the inaugural year of the American League) through 1910, earned him a spot in the Cleveland baseball Hall of Fame.

Tris Speaker, often rated as baseball's greatest centerfielder and a member of virtually every thoughtfully chosen pre-1950 All-time All-Star team (the outfield generally consisted of Cobb, Speaker and Ruth), served the Indians in many capacities from being a play-by-play commentator on TV to batting and outfield coach, was always highly visible in Cleveland.

Cy Young, the winningest pitcher in big league baseball history with 511 victories in a career spanning 22 years (1890–1911), often came up to Cleveland from his Newcomerstown, Ohio, home to take part in all sorts of special ceremonies, including various "Opening Day" festivities.

Young in the 1940s and 1950s was an integral part of the Indians baseball scene, looming as a gigantic historical figure from baseball's "Late Stone Age." Happily enough, he had spent a good part of his career hurling for Cleveland.

As visible as Bradley, Speaker and Cy Young were, hardly anyone bothered them for their autographs. If, hypothetically, they had been cavorting around the ballpark in 1990, they could have hardly moved from "Point A" to "Point B" without being accosted by big name hunters.

Certainly, baseball fans collected autographs 40-odd years ago, but they did so in a more casual way. Nowadays, if a hobbyist goes out and buys a star signature at a card show—such as a Willie Mays, a Joe DiMaggio or a Ted Williams, he knows he can always get his money back by selling it to another collector—and oftentimes for a profit. There was no market and profit motive at all in autograph collecting a generation or two ago.

If anyone had the wit to get a Bradley, Speaker or Cy Young autograph on a baseball 40 years ago, those single signature spheroids would be worth *at least* $1,000 to $2,000 apiece in 1990.

Collectors today are more obsessed with statistics than ever before—and thus you will see them trying to get autographs from "300 Game-Winners," "500-Homer Hitters," "3,000-hit men," etc. on the same baseball.

Though stats have always been the lifeblood of baseball, Tris Speaker once told this writer: "When I got base hit number 3,000 back in 1925 while I was playing with the Indians, the newspaper sports pages only made passing mention of it. Numbers didn't seem to be too important then."

By the same token, Joe Sewell, who came up to the Indians from the New Orleans Pelicans in mid-August 1920 to replace Ray Chapman at shortstop said: "When I played my 1,000th consecutive game for the Indians in 1926, the papers hardly made mention of it. Consecutive game streaks were no big deal then. It was still a long time before Lou Gehrig would come around and set the all-time record at 2,130 games in a row.

The old "Iron Man" record had been held by infielder Everett Scott who had played in 1,307 straight games. The streak came to an end on May 5, 1925 when the New York Yankees benched Scott for weak hitting. (Scott had begun the streak on June 20, 1916 when he was a member of the Boston Red Sox.)

Joe Sewell got up to 1,103 games in a row before he was forced to the sidelines for a couple of days with a bad case of the flu. As good a player as Joe Sewell was, he didn't receive a single vote for the Hall of Fame when balloting for baseball shrine membership was inaugurated in 1936. Over a 14-year career (1920–33), Sewell batted .312, a great average for an infielder, rapped out 2,226 base hits, and struck out only 114 times in more than 8,000 trips to the plate. As a shortstop and third baseman, he was sure-handed, had a strong arm and could make all the plays.

Sewell had to wait until 1977, however, more than 40 years after he had retired from active play, before he finally gained Hall of Fame membership through a vote of the Committee on Baseball Veterans. Over the years Sewell's record in retrospect began to look more and more impressive, deserving a bronze plaque with his portrait hung at the Hall of Fame Gallery in Cooperstown.

After his belated election to the HOF, Sewell became one of the most familiar figures on the autograph circuit, at major baseball events across the U.S.A., including various banquets, Hall of Fame Induction Ceremonies, those official functions surrounding the All-Star Games and World Series. As he approached the age of 90 he had to stop traveling altogether—but this only meant that he could have "private signing" sessions and turn out autographs by the hundreds and thousands.

When he died at the age of 91 early in 1990, Joe Sewell completed a career in baseball that covered nearly 70 years. It was a phenomenon of the 1980s and 1990s that Joe Sewell, like many other oldtime ballplayers, could earn as much cash from a half-dozen or so card show appearances as for an entire season of major league play under the broiling sun.

Joe Sewell and Burleigh Grimes Sign the Same Baseball

In July 1981 at the Hall of Fame Induction Ceremonies at Cooperstown, in wandering through the spacious lobby of the grand old Hotel Otesaga, official hostelry for the "Hall of Fame Weekend," we saw at least a dozen Hall of Famers milling around, including Joe Sewell, who signed a baseball for us.

At the other end of the Otesaga lobby tough old Burleigh Grimes, then 88, was holding court with a group of reporters. We managed to ask Burleigh about his pitching techniques. (When Grimes retired from the big league scene as an active pitcher after the 1934 season, he was the last of the "legal" spitballers.)

The subject was the 1920 World Series between the Brooklyn Dodgers and the Cleveland Indians in which Grimes was a mound stalwart for the Dodgers. Since Grimes had faced Sewell in that series, we had an idea and pulled out the baseball just signed by Sewell and asked Grimes to sign alongside Joey's autograph.

Grimes took the ball, obligingly signed, but as he was finishing we saw his face darken into an expression of outrage. Roared Burleigh: "I never liked that 1920 World Series! We should have beaten the Indians easily, but some of our boys took Cleveland too lightly, celebrated a little too much between games and came to the park a little hung over. And don't ask me to name the guys who misbehaved . . . let 'em rest in peace!" concluded Burleigh as he struggled to control his rage.

Grimes and Sewell were just about the last of the survivors from that Brooklyn-Cleveland meeting of 70 years ago, That's how this baseball, signed by two Hall of Famers, who opposed each other in a long-ago World Series, came to be worth a sum well into four figures.

Babe Ruth-Autographed Ball Saves a Boy's Life

Nowadays a baseball autographed by Babe Ruth brings big bucks on the memorabilia marketplace, but back in 1926 a spheroid autographed by the Bambino actually *saved a boy's life*, or so goes the legend.

In early October 1926 it seems that Johnny Sylvester, an 11-year-old New York City schoolboy and a rabid baseball fan, fell desperately ill and was given only days to live by his doctors. Johnny's family sent out urgent telegrams to both the New York Yankees and St. Louis Cardinals, the two teams engaged in the '26 World Series, to donate autographed baseballs, so that the stricken boy might at least enjoy the waning moments of his life.

Happily, an airmail package containing two balls arrived almost immediately—one signed by the Cardinals team and the other by the "Bronx Bombers," with Ruth's signature appearing on the "Sweet Spot." Included in the package was a special message from Ruth reading: "I'll knock a homer for you on Wednesday."

On that Wednesday October 6th at St. Louis' Sportsman's Park, Ruth came through magnificently for Johnny Sylvester as he slammed out, not one, but three homers in leading the Yankees to a 10–4 rout over the Cards in the fourth game of the Series, which became knotted at two games each.

In a letter dated October 9 and addressed "To my sick little pal" he promised the boy another homer in Game 6 at Yankee Stadium but Ruth failed to deliver, proving that he was not invincible as the Bronx Bombers were drubbed by a 10–2 count.

After the Yanks lost the Series to the Cards in the seventh game, despite a Ruth homer, the Babe made a well-publicized visit to young Sylvester and said, "Johnny, I'm sorry the Yankees didn't win." Nevertheless, the boy made a miraculous recovery from his illness and his father was moved to say, "It was Babe Ruth's autographed ball and personal visit that saved my boy's life."

Reporters could never determine specifically the nature of Johnny's illness, but the range of ailments ascribed to him included blood poisoning, a sinus condition, a spinal fusion and a spinal infection. Another account indicated that the ailment was an infection of the forehead caused by a kick from a horse after the youngster fell while riding in Essex Falls, N.J. His father, Horace C. Sylvester, Jr., a vice president of the National City Bank in New York, maintained an estate there.

A UPI photo published in newspapers throughout the world showed Ruth in uniform standing with Johnny, who had a large bandage on his forehead.

Sylvester went on to graduate from Princeton University in 1937, served as a lieutenant in the U.S. Navy in World War II and later became president of Amscomatic Inc., a manufacturer of packing machinery in Long Island City, N.Y. After Johnny died on Jan. 8, 1990 at the age of 74, the *New York Times* obituary said in part: "There was nothing Mr. Sylvester could have done to match the pinnacle he reached in 1926 when he became the most famous little boy in America."

Bob Feller, Star on the Card Show Circuit

Robert William Andrew "Bob" Feller maintains one of the most active schedules on the card show circuit of any ex-ballplayer. Feller's Hall of Fame status (elected in his first year of eligibility) makes him something special since only two or three dozen HOFers regularly appear at card shows.

Feller broke explosively into the major leagues with the Cleveland Indians in 1936. A 17-year-old flame thrower just off the Iowa farm, he struck out 8 St. Louis Cardinals in just 3 innings of work in an exhibition game. In his first major league start he struck out 15 batters. Before the '36 season was over he equalled the big league one-game strikeout record of 17. He established the all-time strikeout mark (since broken) of 18 in the last game of the '38 season against the Detroit Tigers. By the time he concluded his career after the 1956 season, he had piled up a winning record of 266–162 with 2,581 strikeouts. In 1946, he fanned a record 348 batters, a standard later surpassed only by Sandy Koufax and Nolan Ryan.

Feller's lifetime stats would have been even more impressive had he not spent more than 3½ years in the U.S. Navy during World War II between 1942–1945. He had a most distinguished war record as a combat gunner on the battleship *U.S.S. Alabama*.

Feller, under normal conditions, would have been a sure bet to achieve well over 300 victories and perhaps as many as 4,000 strikeouts, but he emphasizes "I had a good career and am lucky that my right arm held out for 18 years of big league pitching."

At the conclusion of the '46 campaign, when he went 26–15 in an astounding 371 innings of work, he signed a contract with the Indians for $80,000, making him the highest paid player in baseball at the time. And because his career was so extraordinary, Feller continues to be a star at any card show—yet, since he appears at so many of these events (perhaps 40 to 50 a year) his per-autograph price is only a modest $5 to $6. (Hall of Famers who appear at only a scattering of shows get higher fees because their signatures are considered to be "scarce." Harold "Pee Wee" Reese, the Brooklyn Dodgers star shortstop of the 1940s and '50s, appears at only a few selected shows and commands a per-autograph fee of 15 bucks.)

Feller is considered by many of the game's historians as having been the fastest pitcher of all time. Nolan Ryan's fastball has been clocked at 100.9 mph, while Feller in 1946 had his "heater" clocked at a then record of 98.6 mph. Feller at a recent card show said, however: "Measuring equipment is much more sophisticated today . . . if I had been clocked with a laser gun of the type used to measure Ryan's fastball, I strongly believe I would have been clocked at from 105 to 106 miles per hour."

Feller maintains that the clocking should be based on the *average* speed of the ball as it travels from the pitcher's mound to home plate. He said: "When the ball leaves Ryan's hand it travels for a few feet at maybe 117 mph, but by the time it reaches the plate the speed has dropped below 100. The most accurate measure should be based on the average speed the ball travels over that route of 60 feet and 6 inches."

Feller pays tribute to Ryan for maintaining his velocity well into his 40s. "Rapid Robert" said, a bit wistfully: "Just before mid-season in 1947, I fell off the high pitcher's mound at Shibe Park, Philadelphia. I hurt my shoulder and never had the same fastball again. Freak accidents like that happen in baseball all the time."

Feller has written several books, including one released in spring 1990 entitled *Now Pitching*, a tome that covers the old speedballers half-century in the game. He's been making autograph appearances all across the U.S.A. promoting the book. Feller said in this regard: "Most of the fans who line up to get signed copies of my book never saw me pitching big league competition . . . After all, I retired nearly 35 years ago, but true fans are knowledgeable, read baseball history, and many of them see me on the card show circuit."

In 1947, Feller published a best-seller, written in collaboration with Frank Gibbons (then a sportswriter with the *Cleveland Press*), entitled *Strikeout Story*. In mid-season '47, said Feller, "I had an autograph session at the biggest downtown Cleveland bookstore. I signed something like 220 books that day, and at night I had enough strength left to go the distance and beat the Boston Red Sox 2–1."

Reagan Remembers Wrong

In his memoirs, retired House Speaker Thomas "Tip" O'Neill recalled conferring with President Ronald Reagan in the White House Oval Office when the conversation turned to Grover Cleveland, the nation's 22nd and 24th president. "Oh, Grover Cleveland, I played him in the movies," commented Reagan.

"Oh, no, you didn't, Mr. President," declared the astonished House Speaker. "You played the part of Grover Cleveland Alexander, the ballplayer.

The Strange Case of Pete Rose

Pete Rose got himself into trouble when he sold the Phillies uniform he wore on the historic occasion when he set a National League record for most hits in 1981 to a collector for a figure close to $10,000.

When Phillies management heard about this action—which they considered to be "profiteering"—they fined Rose the amount of money he received for that uniform. From a technical standpoint, the uniform was Phillies property to begin with.

A player usually wears no more than one complete uniform during the course of any given game, so for Pete to wear six or more on one day is absolutely ridiculous. Yet this many uniforms have come onto the memorabilia market.

As to the authenticity of a game uniform worn during a milestone performance, we must often rely solely on the probity of the player involved. In the case of Pete Rose's uniforms, he may not have been entirely forthcoming. Actions of this type seriously damage the entire baseball memorabilia market.

Over the years, Pete Rose has sold off some of his most outstanding personal trophies, including his diamond-studded Hickock Belt (awarded in 1981 for being chosen as the top professional athlete of the year) and the $25,000 Waterford Crystal set he received from *The Sporting News* as the "Man of the Year" for 1985. The latter award was presented to him for breaking Ty Cobb's all-time hit record. For selling these prized trophies, Pete Rose received boxcar sums of money.

As Rose was approaching the Ty Cobb base hit milestone, he was literally a national hero, a symbol of baseball at its best. On the magical evening in the summer of '85 when he stroked out hit number 4,192 he received a congratulatory phone call from President Ronald Reagan who was ensconced in his White House Oval Office. That sort of thing is almost enough to turn anyone's head.

Also, when Pete broke Ty Cobb's hallowed 4,191 hit record he was presented with a beautiful shiny red Corvette by General Motors. Rose promptly sold the Corvette for $55,000 (the car was touted as a rare bit of memorabilia) because by this time he was in a serious financial bind due to astronomical gambling debts.

As to the sale of the car, Rose testified: "I had three Porsches and a Rolls Royce. So what the hell do I need a Corvette for?"

At about the same time Rose sold the Corvette, he also sold his bat and ball that were involved in breaking Cobb's record.

Rose's Card Show Appearances

Rose became one of the most popular figures at card shows where literally hundreds of fans would line up for his autograph. Throughout the 1980s, Rose generally made between $8,000 and $12,000 for each card show appearance. He insisted continuously that he be paid in cash. On one occasion a show promoter gave Rose a check and Pete screamed, "I told you I wanted cash!"

However, the ever-watchful U.S. Internal Revenue Service did take careful notice of Rose's financial shenanigans and discovered that he failed to report many hundreds of thousands of dollars of income from the sale of memorabilia and card show appearances. He was sent to jail.

Foiled Again!

The island of Grenada came out in 1988 with nine miniature souvenir sheets, each consisting of nine postage stamps, portraying a total of 81 major league baseball players, both past and present. Each stamp is denominated at 30 cents (Grenada) and all the stamps could ostensibly be used for postal purposes on this little Caribbean isle, though they were obviously produced primarily for collectors. Pete Rose, then a star of the Cincinnati Reds, appears on one of the sheets. (See color section.)

Grenada wanted to reprint all the sheets in 1990 in order to allow five large American supermarket chains to offer the stamps as part of a promotional effort. However, Major League Baseball, through Commissioner Fay Vincent's office, requested that the Pete Rose stamp be withdrawn from the reprint issue, a request that the government of Grenada granted. Major League Baseball's clout comes from having lent its name and logo to the entire stamp issue and it draws royalties from the sales.

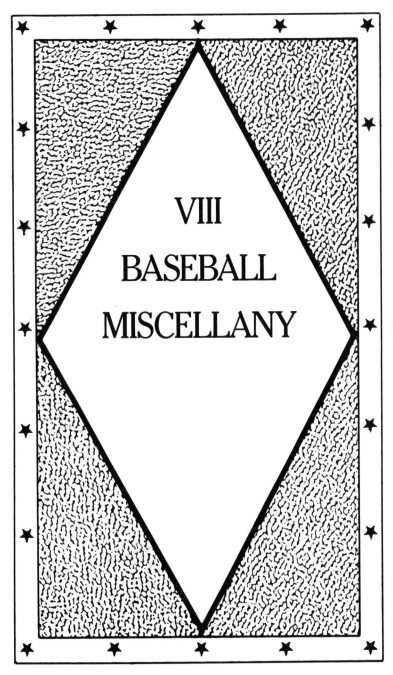

VIII

BASEBALL

MISCELLANY

Grading Baseball Cards

Baseball cards these days are as carefully graded as are stamps and coins. Most collectors and dealers now consider six grades of cards as being collectible. Here is an outline summary of those six grades as enumerated by Krause Publications (Iola, Wisconsin) which produces a number of baseball memorabilia periodicals, including *Baseball Cards Magazine*, *Baseball Card News* and *Sports Collectors Digest*.

Fair (*F*): A complete card, but one that contains damage such as writing on card back, tack holes, and heavy creases.

Good (*G*): A well-worn card, but one that exhibits no intentional damage. May have major or multiple creases. Corners may be rounded well beyond card border.

Very Good (*VG*): Shows obvious handling. May have rounded corners, minor creases, moderate gum or wax stains. No major creases, tape marks, writing, etc.

Excellent (*EX*): Corners are still fairly sharp with only moderate wear. Borders may be off-center. No creases or stains on fronts or backs, but may show slight loss of surface luster.

Near Mint (*NR MT*): A nearly perfect card. At first glance, a NR MT card appears to be perfect. May have one corner not perfectly sharp. May be slightly off-center. No surface marks, creases, or loss of gloss.

Mint (*MT*): A perfect card. Well-centered with all corners sharp and square. No creases, stains, edge nicks, surface marks, yellowing or fading, regardless of age.

A card's condition will have a great deal of bearing, of course, on its value. For example, a 1987 Fleer Will Clark card (No. 269) is currently quoted at $27.00 in Near Mint and at $35.00 in Mint—and over the years the Mint specimen will appreciate at a far more rapid rate than the Near Mint card. The same Will Clark card in Fair to Good might bring only $1 or $2. Sophisticated card collectors and investors concern themselves seriously with the condition factor.

A Lefty Grove Diamond Stars 1934 (No. 1) may well bring over $1,000 in Near Mint or Mint, but in Fair to Good it may be worth only a few dollars.

The famed Honus Wagner Sweet Caporal Cigarettes T-206, *c.* 1910, is extremely difficult to find in Near Mint to Mint, but when the Wagner does show up in those superior grades it brings over $100,000 at either public auction or private treaty sale. The Wagner T-206 in the lower grades is worth far far less.

Basic Baseball Books

Baseball books make up one of the most important groups of diamond game memorabilia, and here we've given an annotated bibliography of 10 of the most widely read baseball tomes published within the past generation.

In writing this section we've consulted Mike Shannon's *Diamond Classics: Essays on 100 of the Best Baseball Books Ever Published* (Jefferson, N.C.: McFarland & Co., Inc., 1989), 455pp., $25.00.

We've arranged our list of 10 books alphabetically according to title.

From a personal standpoint, these are among the liveliest and most interesting books we've read in recent years. Moreover, they're easily available at most public libraries.

THE ARMCHAIR BOOK OF BASEBALL, John Thorn, Editor, New York: Charles Scribner's Sons, 1985. Cloth, 388pp. Foreword by Peter Ueberroth.

John Thorn's book is one of the best anthologies of the diamond game published in recent years. It contains 61 pieces by 61 different authors. Representative selections include: Don Hoak, "The Day I Batted Against Castro;" Bart Giamatti, "The Green Fields of the Mind;" John Kieran, "Was There Ever a Guy Like Ruth?;" Donald Hall, "Baseball and the Meaning of Life;" Wilfred Sheed, "Notes on the Country Game;" and George Will, "The Chicago Cubs, Overdue."

BABE: THE LEGEND COMES TO LIFE, Robert W. Creamer, New York: Simon and Schuster, 1974. Cloth, 443pp.

The publication of *Babe* was timed to take advantage of renewed interest in Ruth brought on by Henry Aarons' inevitable passing of Ruth in the lifetime home run derby in 1974. *Time* magazine for August 26, 1974 commented that Creamer's work was the first really adult biography of the Babe, as well as one of the best, and least sentimental, books.

Creamer tells the Babe's story fully and skillfully. Ruth was more than the greatest player of the game; he was, and still is today, more famous and vastly more popular than most U.S. Presidents. George Herman Ruth was an American original.

BALL FOUR: MY LIFE AND HARD TIMES THROWING THE KNUCKLEBALL IN THE BIG LEAGUES, Jim Bouton, Edited by Leonard Shecter, New York and Cleveland: The World Publishing Co., 1970, Cloth, 400pp.

Jim Bouton concentrates mostly on the 1969 season when he divided his time between pitching for the American League expansion team, the Seattle Pilots, and the National League's Houston Astros. Said Rex Lardner in his review of *Ball Four* for the *New York Times*: "Irreverent Jim Bouton! Betrayer of secrets! Clubhouse lawyer! Doesn't care whom he converts into enemies. Sly practical joker. Weirdo who throws baseball's most weirdo pitch—the knuckleball. . . . And in *Ball Four* . . . Bouton has written the funniest, frankest book yet about the species 'ballplayer satyriaticus' and his numerous bosses, most of whom come out pretty stuffy. . . ."

Commented Roger Angell in *The New Yorker*: "*Ball Four* should be celebrated as the most intelligent and entertaining participant's account of the national pastime yet published."

BASEBALL AS I HAVE KNOWN IT, Fred Lieb, New York: Coward McCann & Geoghegan, Inc., 1977. Cloth, 288pp.

Lieb, author of more than 40 baseball books, wrote this as he approached his 90th birthday. He began following baseball when there was only one major league and finished his career when there were 26 big league teams.

Said Cincinnati writer Mike Shannon: "The smell and feel of

dozens of old ballparks and press boxes long gone from the American scene are imprinted on the pages, but the freshness and immediacy of the book will last as long as anyone who knows the names of Cobb, Ruth and Gehrig."

THE BASEBALL ENCYCLOPEDIA: THE COMPLETE AND OFFICIAL RECORD OF MAJOR LEAGUE BASEBALL, 7th Edition, Joseph L. Reichler, Editor. New York: Macmillan, 1988. Cloth, 2,875pp.
Complete batting and pitching statistics for every player who participated in at least one major league game since 1876. Also complete rosters of major league managers and their records.

BASEBALL'S GREAT EXPERIMENT: JACKIE ROBINSON AND HIS LEGACY, Jules Tygiel, New York: Oxford University Press, 1983. Cloth.
Observed the *Library Journal*: "Tygiel's intelligence, insight, and exemplary yet equitable candor command one's attention; not a facet of civil rights issues passes without his incisive commentary. His book is a definitive statement."

THE BOYS OF SUMMER, Roger Kahn, New York: Harper & Row Publishers, 1971. Cloth, 442pp.
In *The Boys of Summer*, one of the best-selling sports books of all time, Roger Kahn immortalizes the Brooklyn Dodgers of the 1950s.

EIGHT MEN OUT: THE BLACK SOX AND THE 1919 WORLD SERIES, Eliot Asinof, New York: Holt Rinehart and Winston, 1963. Cloth, 302pp.
This is by far the finest book ever written on the 1919 World Series scandal . . . reads like a novel.

THE GLORY OF THEIR TIMES, Lawrence Ritter, New York: Macmillan, 1966. Cloth, 300pp.
Ritter tape-recorded interviews with 22 ballplayers prominent in the first quarter of the 20th century. His interviewing techniques have been adapted on a universal scale.

THE GREAT AMERICAN BASEBALL CARD FLIPPING, TRADING AND BUBBLE GUM BOOK, Brendan C. Boyd and Fred C. Harris, Boston: Little, Brown, 1973. Cloth, 151pp.
This is the first book-length treatment of baseball cards. The

central theme revolves around the author's contention that base-ball card collecting often constitutes a very meaningful aspect of American childhood culture.

A SPECIAL REPORT TO THE COMMISSIONER OF BASEBALL IN THE MATTER OF PETER EDWARD ROSE, better known as THE DOWD REPORT (prepared by attorney John Dowd), published May 9, 1989.

This is the biggest, heaviest and most expensive baseball book ever written and published. The "outline" volume alone (priced at $30) runs to 225 pages, while the 8 volumes of "evidence" (priced at $200 per set) total 2,447 pages. The 9 volumes together weigh more than 60 pounds.

The Dowd Report deals specifically with Pete Rose's gambling on major league baseball during the 1985–87 period, and the conclusion is that "Charlie Hustle" bet on 442 games in that span, more than 50 times on Cincinnati (the team managed by Rose). That was enough to cause the late Baseball Commissioner, Dr. Bart Giamatti, to boot Pete out of Organized Baseball for life.

Newspapers and Magazines

Baseball Cards Magazine (monthly), $15.95 per year
Krause Publications, 700 E. State St., Iola, Wisc. 54990

Baseball Card News (bi-weekly), $23.95 per year
P.O. Box 2510, Del Mar, Calif. 92014

Baseball Hobby News (monthly), $15.95 per year
4540 Kearny Villa Rd., San Diego, Calif. 92123

Canadian Sportscard Collector (monthly), $15.95 per year
103 Lakeshore Rd., St. Catharines, Ontario, Canada L2N 2T6

Sports Collectors Digest (weekly), $39.95 per year
Krause Publications, 700 E. State St., Iola, Wisc. 54990

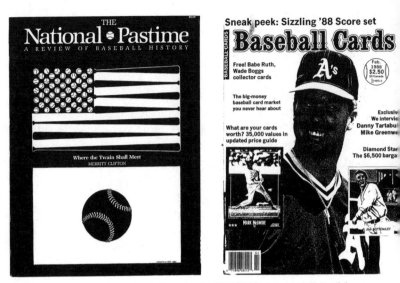

The Society for Baseball Research ("SABR") has published hundreds of books and monographs on every phase of the diamond game within the past 20 years. The National Pastime *is SABR's annual "Review of Baseball History."* Baseball Cards *magazine, published monthly by Krause Publications, Iola, Wisc., enjoys a circulation of nearly 200,000.*

The cover for the National Baseball Hall of Fame & Museum 1990 Yearbook *features stylized portraits of the new inductees for 1990, Joe Morgan and Jim Palmer, by the noted baseball artist LeRoy Neiman.*

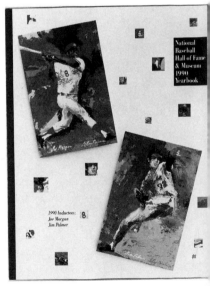

Baseball Hall of Fame Yearbooks Rank as Prized Collectors' Items

"If you saw him play, you'll never forget him. No one ran with such hurried grace. His gifts as an athlete were marvelous because they were subdued.

"Here was an outfielder who followed a ball with a deft serenity as though his progress had been plotted by a choreographer concerned only with the defeat of awkwardness."—Jimmy Cannon, *New York Journal-American*.

This is how the late great sportswriter Jimmy Cannon summed up the talents of Joe DiMaggio in a single brief paragraph, and this is only one of hundreds of quotations recalling the achievements of the 206 Hall of Famers to be found in the National Baseball Hall of Fame and Museum's *Yearbook* for 1990.

In recent years the HOF *Yearbook* has grown from 92 to 140 pages, with backstrip for easy shelfing, and is now considered as an authentic collector's item.

The quotations by and about Hall of Famers make the *Yearbook* a joy to read: A few others:

"Hitting is timing. Pitching is upsetting timing."—Warren Spahn.

"I'd rather pitch to any other hitter in the league. He's bad news all the time. No game is ever won against the Cardinals until Joe Medwick is out in the ninth"—Van Lingle Mungo.

"Every time I sign a baseball, and there must have been thousands, I thank my luck that I wasn't born Coveleski or Wambsganss or Peckinpaugh."—Mel Ott.

"Don't alibi on bad hops. Anybody can stop the good ones."—Joe McCarthy.

"Jimmie Foxx wasn't scouted, he was trapped."—Lefty Gomez.

"Babe Ruth and Old Jack Dempsey, both Sultans of the Swat.

One hits where other people are—the other where they're not."—
John Lardner, *Chicago Tribune*.

"I never saw a pitcher I didn't think I could hit. To tell the truth,
I felt sorry for most of the poor slobs trying to get me out."—
Rogers Hornsby.

A special feature in the *Yearbook* is titled "I Wish I Would
Have Been There," in which an array of Hall of Famers answer
the question, "Which special event in baseball history have you
not personally witnessed but wished you had?"

Some of the answers include:

"When Bill Mazeroski hit his dramatic seventh game, ninth
inning homer to defeat the Yankees in the 1960 World Series.
Pittsburgh went crazy."—Edd Roush.

"When Mickey Mantle homered off the facade at Yankee Stadium. I don't think I ever saw one hit that far. It came the closest
to being the only fair ball ever hit out of Yankee Stadium."—Ted
Williams.

A major feature of the *Yearbook* consists of the 500-odd photographs, with more than half in color. Many of the photos are of
items in the Hall of Fame Museum, including baseball cards
(from the early cigarette types of the 1880s and 1890s to contemporary Topps cards).

It's possible for the baseball fan to take a vicarious tour of the
Hall of Fame exhibit areas by paging through the '90 *Yearbook*.

Dozens of Hall of Famers are depicted via baseball card portraits, e.g.: Adrian C. "Cap" Anson and James "Pud" Galvin on the
"Old Judge" cigarette cards, c. 1888; Babe Ruth, Luke Appling
and Bobby Doerr on the 1930s Goudey gum cards; Honus Wagner on the famous "Sweet Caporal" cigarette card of 1910; George
Kell on a Bowman gum card, c. 1950; Joe Morgan on a 1970s
Topps gum card; and Johnny Bench on a 1980s Leaf-Donruss
gum card.

The Hall of Fame *Yearbook* also features an array of noteworthy baseball paintings, including stylized portraits of the HOF
inductees for '90, Joe Morgan and Jim Palmer, by the noted baseball artist LeRoy Neiman (front cover) and "Three Umpires" by
Norman Rockwell. The HOF *Yearbook* is a bargain at $8.

Ticket Stubs

A Dodger Stadium field box seat for the June 8, 1968 game between Los Angeles and Philadelphia in which Don Drysdale's record steak of 58 scoreless innings came to an end.

An unused full ticket to the scheduled first night game in Chicago Cubs history, Wrigley Field, August 8, 1988, Cubs vs. Phillies. The game was postponed due to rain and was re-scheduled for the following evening. The donation was made by the late Baseball Commissioner A. Bartlett Giamatti.

Ticket stub to Game 4 of the 1971 World Series played on October 6 at Three Rivers Stadium, Pittsburgh. This was the first night game in World Series history.

"Writer Cards"

Authors of baseball books are now being portrayed on cards that are patterned after bubble-gum cards. The Writer Cards are the brainchild of Mike Shannon, publisher of *Spitball: The Literary Baseball Magazine*. Thus far, eight cards have been produced in *Spitball's* first series, with 16 more due shortly in the second and third series.

John Holway "gave us the pioneering *Voices from the Great Black Baseball Leagues*. Won the 1988 Casey Award for *Blackball Stars*," says the inscription on Holway's "All-Star Authors" card. Holway followed up his 1975 book, *Voices*, with *Blackball Stars*, about the old Negro professional baseball leagues.

In addition to the Holway card, writers portrayed in the first series are: Charles Alexander, *Ty Cobb* and *John McGraw*. Charles Einstein, *Fireside Book of Baseball* series and *Willie's Time*. Peter Golenbock, *The Bronx Zoo* and *Bums* (a 1984 Casey Award winner). Bill James, *Historical Baseball Abstract* (a 1986 Casey winner). W. P. Kinsella, *Shoeless Joe* and *Iowa Baseball Confederacy*. Daniel Okrent, *The Ultimate Baseball Book*, co-editor, and *Nine Innings*.

JOHN HOLWAY

Gave us the pioneering *Voices From the Great Black Baseball Leagues.* Won the 1988 Casey Award for *Blackball Stars*

DANIEL OKRENT

Co-editor of sumptuous *The Ultimate Baseball Book,* Dan also authored the fine study, *Nine Innings.*

CHARLES EINSTEIN

Compiler of the landmark *Fireside Book of Baseball* series, Charles also penned a great baseball biography, *Willie's Time.*

JIM BROSNAN

An excellent reliever, "The Professor" showed that jocks can have smarts. Ghostless, he wrote two classic best-sellers: *The Long Season & Pennant Race*

Prominent authors of books on baseball are now being portrayed on "All-Star Writer Cards," created by Mike Shannon, publisher of Spitball *Magazine. "It's time we give baseball writers their proper due," says Shannon.*

PETER GOLENBOCK

Wrote bb book which had longest stay on NY Times Book Review best sellers list: *The Bronx Zoo.* Won 1984 Casey for *Bums.*

Other writers definitely scheduled to appear in the *Spitball* series are Roger Kahn, Donald Honig, John Thorn, David Voight and Robert Obojski.

Jim Brosnan is the only writer in the *Spitball* series who has also been portrayed in a baseball card set. Brosnan, who pitched in the majors from 1954 to 1963 appears on a variety of baseball cards, especially in the Topps annual series.

The inscription on Brosnan's card reads: "An excellent reliever, 'The Professor' showed that jocks can have smarts. Ghostless, he wrote two classic best-sellers: *The Long Season* and *Pennant Race.*"

Commented Shannon: "The main purpose of the cards is to provide more recognition for these truly fine authors."

The cards are inserted in strips of two into *Spitball.* The only way to get them is by subscribing to this quarterly journal ($12 a year), 4224 Collegevue Place, Cincinnati, Ohio 45224. Shannon admits he got the insert idea from the monthly *Baseball Cards Magazine* (produced by Krause Publications), which includes color card inserts of big league players.

Pat Spencer's Series of Baseball Dolls

Doll collecting, within the past decade, has become one of the fastest-growing and most popular of all hobbies. . . . and modern dollmakers have discovered along the way that dolls related to baseball have particular interest to specialists in diamond game memorabilia.

In this respect, Pat Spencer, who is based in Cooperstown, N.Y., home of the Baseball Hall of Fame, has been turning out one of the most successful series of baseball dolls ever produced. (Pat is the wife of Ted Spencer, Chief Curator at the HOF.)

Her first major effort in this area came in 1986 when she completed her "Cooperstown Bicentennial Doll," a creation that marked the 200th anniversary of the founding of Cooperstown, that picturesque village on the shores of Lake Otsego in upstate New York. Standing 18 inches high, the doll is hand-painted, has a boy's face, and wears a baseball uniform of 1880s vintage with an ornate "C" inscribed across the shirt front. Pat used an actual major league uniform of that period (one taken from the HOF archives) as a model. The doll comes in a limited edition of 200, and a few specimens are still available at the HOF Gift Shop. All of Pat Spencer's baseball dolls, in fact, come in limited editions.

Her next effort came a year later with the title of the "Leatherstocking Town Ball Doll." Town ball was a relatively primitive form of baseball played in the Cooperstown area in the mid-19th century. This creation, also standing 18 inches high, wears authentic period clothes—cap, drop-front trousers, drop-shoulder shirt and tied scarf. This doll, with its porcelain head, hands and feet, harks back to the "roots" of baseball.

In 1988, Pat Spencer came out with a set of two dolls, one depicting the "Mighty Casey," and the other his girlfriend "Merry." This set was inspired both by Ernest Thayer's famous 1888 poem "Casey at the Bat," and on the recently written operetta by William Schumann about the legendary "Mudville" slugger. "Merry," while not mentioned in the Thayer poem, plays a major role in the Schumann operetta.

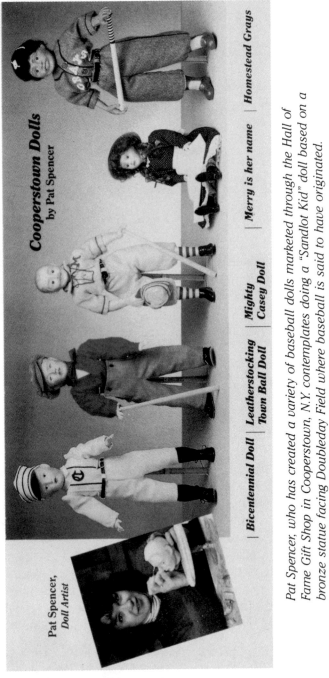

Cooperstown Dolls
by Pat Spencer

Pat Spencer,
Doll Artist

| Bicentennial Doll | Leatherstocking Town Ball Doll | Mighty Casey Doll | Merry is her name | Homestead Grays |

Pat Spencer, who has created a variety of baseball dolls marketed through the Hall of Fame Gift Shop in Cooperstown, N.Y. contemplates doing a "Sandlot Kid" doll based on a bronze statue facing Doubleday Field where baseball is said to have originated.

Casey is dressed in a faithful reproduction of an 1890s uniform that is tailored of fine wool challis. He stands 18 inches high, while Merry measures 16 inches. Casey holds his cap in his right hand and a wooden bat in his left.

Merry, the faithful girlfriend, wears a vintage 1890s costume, lace-trimmed at the neck and sleeves, while a straw skimmer tops her auburn braids. Both Casey and Merry come in limited editions of 100.

Early in 1990, Pat Spencer completed her "The Grays" doll which pays tribute to all men who played in the Negro Professional Baseball Leagues. Standing the usual 18 inches in height, the doll wears an all-wool uniform (inscribed "Grays" across the shirt front), cap (with a "G" logo), leather belt and holds a wooden bat in his hands. The head, hands and feet are finely sculpted porcelain, the body is of jointed composition construction, while the eyes are glass paperweight.

Only 100 "Grays" are being made, each one signed and numbered by the artist.

Each of the dolls is priced at $225.00, but the Hall of Fame is offering the set of 5 for an even $1,000. According to present plans, the sixth number in Pat Spencer's Cooperstown Doll Collection will be titled "The Sandlot Kid." She'll base this creation on the lifesize bronze statue of the same name which is displayed on a pedestal at the driveway entrance to Doubleday Field, Cooperstown.

"The Sandlot Kid," who stands barefoot with a bat in his hands (he's a righthanded swinger), wears a broad-brimmed hat and a typical farm-boy outfit. "I want my doll to be faithful to the spirit of the statue, even to the 'Sandlot Kid's' choke grip," says Pat Spencer.

All of Pat's baseball dolls thus far wear the old-fashioned uniforms consisting of bulky woolen flannels . . . it wasn't until the late 1960s and early 1970s that form-fitting double-knit polyesters came into vogue in professional baseball. She is in an excellent position to gain any information required on vintage uniforms since her husband Ted takes particular interest in garb worn by ballplayers of all eras.

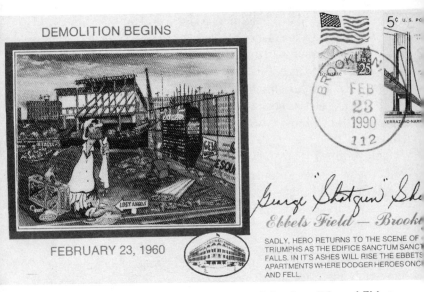

FEBRUARY 23, 1960

SADLY, HERO RETURNS TO THE SCENE OF
TRIUMPHS AS THE EDIFICE SANCTUM SANCT
FALLS. IN IT'S ASHES WILL RISE THE EBBETS
APARTMENTS WHERE DODGER HEROES ONCE
AND FELL.

Commemorating the 30th anniversary of the demolition of Ebbets Field, George "Shotgun" Shuba, one of the renowned "Boys of Summer," autographed this cover, postmarked Feb. 23, 1990 at Brooklyn, N.Y. The Dodgers "Bum," originally drawn by cartoonist Willard Mullin, is seen carrying his suitcase and heading for Los Angeles.

Comiskey Park Goes "On Sale," Brick-by-Brick and Seat-by-Seat

Comiskey Park, built in 1910 on Chicago's South Side, ranked, through 1990, as the oldest continuously used ballyard in the major leagues. However, once the 1990 season came to a close, the wrecker's ball began doing its grisly job. (The brand-new Comiskey Park, located just across the road from old Comiskey, at West 35th Street and the Dan Ryan Expressway, was targeted for completion before the start of the '91 season.)

The seats, bricks, and other parts of the facility that can be salvaged as souvenirs were offered to Chisox season ticket holders first—and anything left over was scheduled to be sold on the public auction block.

Old ballpark seats stand as one of the most popular of any

type of sports collectible. When old Yankee Stadium was torn down in 1972 to make way for an entirely new ballpark, the seats were sold for a few dollars each. Inscribed metal plaques were attached to each seat sold. Within the past few years, a number of these slat-type seats have been appearing on the public sports auction block for $750 to $1,000 per seat.

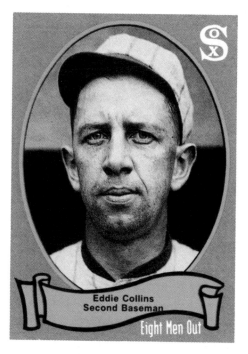

This uniform worn by Eddie Collins in 1917 is the vintage type of Chicago White Sox jerseys specially reproduced for "Turn Back the Clock Day" staged at Comiskey Park on July 11, 1990.

Eddie Collins
Second Baseman

Eight Men Out

Japanese ticket for 200 yen is for a grandstand seat for a Giants game at Korakuen, and carries advertising for an oil firm on the reverse.

Baseball Memorabilia in Japan

Americans may not realize that baseball has been played in Japan since the 1870s when American college teams came by sea to Japan to play exhibition matches and give instructions on the intricacies of the diamond game. In 1878, the University of Wisconsin's varsity nine sailed to Japan to play a series of games against various university teams in Tokyo. During the next 20-odd years many American collegiate teams including Chicago, Stanford, Harvard, California, Washington, Indiana and Illinois universities, traveled across the Pacific to take on Japanese students in baseball.

While college teams kept coming steadily for exhibition tours in Nippon, it was the visits of the U.S. professional organizations that eventually had the deepest impact. In the fall and winter of 1908–09, A. J. Reach & Co., the large U.S. sporting goods manufacturers, who at the time manufactured almost every ball used in the American major and minor leagues, sponsored a squad called the Reach All-American Team, and promoted the trip not only to increase baseball interest in Japan but also to develop an Oriental market for sporting goods.

The Reach All-American team, which included players both from the Pacific Coast League and from both "major" leagues played 19 games against a variety of Japanese college and amateur All-Star teams. They easily won all 19 matches. However, the Americans coached their opponents in the finer points of the game so that the Japanese had a real opportunity to improve upon their baseball skills.

During the next quarter-century various contingents of American professionals visited Japan to both play exhibitions and give instructions, but the "American League Stars" tour in the fall of 1934 was the one of enormous importance.

The delegation was led by Connie Mack, venerable manager of the Philadelphia Athletics, but the team on the field was managed by Babe Ruth of the New York Yankees, who also held the right field spot. The rest of the roster consisted of the following: Lou Gehrig, New York Yankees, first base; Charlie Gehringer, Detroit Tigers, second base; Eric "Boob" McNair, Philadelphia Athletics, shortstop; Jimmie Foxx, Athletics, third base; Frank Hayes, Athletics, and Moe Berg, Cleveland Indians, catchers; Earl Averill, Indians, Edmund "Bing" Miller, Athletics, and Frank "Lefty" O'Doul, recently of the New York Giants, outfielders; Harold "Rabbit" Warstler, Athletics, utility infield; pitchers: Vernon "Lefty" Gomez, Yankees; Joe Cascarella, Clint Brown, Indians, and Earl Whitehill, Washington Senators.

Lefty O'Doul, then 37, who had just signed to manage the San Francisco Seals, had toured Japan previously and was considered one of the delegation's leaders.

The American League Stars played 16 games against the All-Nippon Stars, a team composed mostly of collegiate and corporation team amateur players, and won every one of the games. In the U.S., this imposing team would have probably had an unbeaten record too.

In addition to the 16 games in which the Japanese met the Americans head on, there were two encounters when the players were pooled so that each team was half Japanese and half American. Total attendance for the 18 games ran to almost 500,000—a virtual sell-out for each game wherever it was played.

A classic game was played on Nov. 20, 1934, at Shizuoka. Earl Whitehill, the starting pitcher, found himself locked in a tight pitching duel with Eiji Sawamura, a sensational 18-year-old right-hander, considered the best moundsman in Japan. Sawamura, who had a good fastball, a deceptive curve and plenty of confidence on the mound, struck out a flock of Americans, including Babe Ruth twice, and Gehringer, Ruth, Gehrig and Foxx in order. He battled the visitors to a scoreless tie until the ninth inning, when Lou Gehrig straightened one of his curves into a long home run, and won the game, 1–0.

As a team in the series the Americans batted .326 and banged out 224 base hits, including 37 doubles, 2 triples and 47 homers in those 16 games. They outscored their opponents 193 to 42.

The mighty Babe Ruth led everybody in individual statistics. He slammed out 31 hits, including 13 homers and three doubles, and batted a fat .408. He homered once for every 6 official times at bat.

Averill ranked second in the homer derby with 8, while Foxx belted 7 four-baggers and Gehrig 6.

The Japanese had never seen power hitting of this magnitude before; they even packed the parks well before game time so they could watch Ruth, Gehrig, Foxx, Averill, et al, hit balls into the bleacher seats and over the fences in batting practice. During their stay in Tokyo the American League stars were driven in a motorcade through the city's Ginza District, with Japanese fans of all ages especially eager to get a close-up view of Ruth. The Babe's car was literally mobbed by the throng and the greatest Yankee of them all loved every minute of the street demonstrations.

On this trip, Ruth, 39—or perhaps a little older, since the date of his birth has always been a question mark—actually made his last hurrah in a Yankee uniform. In Feb. 1935, New York handed him his unconditional release, freeing him to sign a contract with the Boston Braves. Ruth played a few games with the Braves and then retired from major league competition for

(Left) Poster featuring Babe Ruth was used to advertise the 1934 tour of U.S. big leaguers. (Above) Japanese cards have been portraying their professional ballplayers for more than a quarter century, but they haven't caught on big with American collectors because they're inscribed in Japanese only.

good. The Babe's eyesight, among other faculties, had declined markedly.

Ruth was so taken with the fierce enthusiasm of the Japanese fans, however, that he expended every bit of his physical strength and competitive spirit to give one of the best slugging performances of his long and illustrious career.

The Japanese people never forgot Ruth: when they built their own Baseball Hall of Fame at Tokyo's Korakuen Stadium, they included as prize exhibits many large photos of Ruth in action in Japanese parks, as well as a variety of Ruthian memorabilia that included one of his bats, a glove, a cap, and autographed balls. For all intents and purposes, The Babe is an unofficial member of their Hall of Fame because his presence there is very real.

Memorabilia from the 1934 Tour

A coterie of sophisticated collectors specializes in gathering material from the American League Stars 1934 tour of Japan. For example, Lefty O'Doul kept an elaborate scrapbook of the entire sojourn. Leather-bound, it contained numerous autographed photos, letters, game programs and related material. After O'Doul's death in 1969, his estate eventually sold off many of his effects including that scrapbook, which became the property of a prominent New York hobby publisher.

An item like the O'Doul scrapbook is valued at many thousands of dollars. Large size posters inscribed in Japanese and featuring a portrait of Ruth wearing a Yankees cap, used to advertise the 1934 tour, are eagerly sought after—and those in good condition can bring prices running well into four figures on those rare occasions when they're offered for sale.

Programs from the various games are also highly valued, especially if they're inscribed with the signatures of any of the players who participated in the tour, American or Japanese.

Newspaper and magazine clippings—both American and Japanese—telling the story of the tour are worthwhile collectibles. New York City in the mid-1930s had some dozen daily newspapers in operation, and many of them covered the tour in great detail in word and photo.

Earl Averill's Sword

Most of the American players on the '34 tour of Japan picked up a personal memento or two and brought them back home, but none of them matched the sheer magnitude of the trophy that centerfielder Earl Averill received. But let's start this story from the beginning.

A game played toward the end of the tour revealed quite graphically the enthusiasm the Japanese have for baseball. Rain fell the night before the game, and continued steadily as game time approached. The fans, however, weren't ready to allow bad weather to prevent them from seeing a contest they'd been eagerly anticipating, particularly since this was the only appearance the two teams would make in Kokura.

Fans began lining up at the gates outside the park at 5 a.m. and when the gates opened around noon some 11,000 persons had "bleacher" tickets. The catch was that there were no seats in the bleachers, which consisted only of bare outfield turf. Also, the outfield was by then ankle deep in water and the hardy "bleacherites" had to stand, kneel, or squat in the shallow lake for the entire game. The total attendance reached 20,000, counting the 9,000 fans in permanent seats in the stands. The enthusiastic fans saw a well-played contest despite the inconveniences, and for the first time got a chance to view close up some of the big American stars, Babe Ruth, Lou Gehrig, and the others.

One spectator, a middle-aged shopkeeper, walked some 80 miles from his home village to see the game at Kokura, and he carried a sword which he vowed to give to the first American smashing a home run against the All-Nippon Stars. This valuable trophy was won by Earl Averill, who connected for a homer early in the contest. It was the highest possible honor he could have received: among the Japanese, a sword was not only a weapon, but also the warrior's badge of honor—it was thought to be his very soul.

We had the opportunity in 1981 to interview Earl Averill, "The Rock of Snohomish," and the first question we asked him was: "Mr. Averill, do you still have that sword a Japanese fan gave you in Kokura in 1934?" After he exhibited surprise that the story of the sword was known in 1981, he said: "I've treasured that Japanese sword for all these years and kept it in a glass trophy case that I had specially built. A couple of years ago I moved the trophy case over to my son Earl Jr.'s house in Snohomish to make sure it will stay in the family. Only my Hall of Fame plaque means as much to me as that sword."

Japanese Baseball Cards and Tickets

Within the past 20 years or so attractive multicolored cards have been produced in Japan showing all players in the Central and Pacific Leagues. These can't be properly called "Bubblegum Cards" because no chewing gum is ever included with them. The cards, measuring 2×3 inches (about the same size as their

American counterparts) are usually encased in blue paper holders. The American collector will need some help in identifying the players portrayed because all inscriptions are in Japanese. Youngsters in Japan collect baseball cards as avidly as do youngsters in the U.S.

American collectors using a little imagination can build up series of cards of American players who saw major league action in both countries, issued by both Japanese and U.S. companies.

A special category might consist of those cards depicting American players who started their careers in the U.S., went to Japan for a stretch, and then came back to the U.S. to resume their careers in the States either as players, coaches or managers. In this category we have men like Clete Boyer, Don Zimmer, Jay Johnstone, Dave Johnson, Larry Doby, Jim Lefebvre, Jim Marshall, and Dick Stuart.

As we've indicated in other sections of this book, ticket stubs (or whole tickets) constitute one of the most important elements of baseball memorabilia collecting.

A comprehensive collection of Japanese ticket stubs can easily reflect the entire history of baseball in the Land of the Rising Sun. These 1908 exhibition series tickets are extremely scarce and valuable as are those of the American League Stars' tours because most were simply thrown out. Ticket stubs from any of the Japan Series also carry substantial premium values. Many of the Japanese tickets are close to being miniature works of art since they are often multicolored and feature a wide array of distinctive vignettes ranging from native birds, stylized baseballs, mythological figures, players in action, stadium facades, etc. Moreover, most of the Japanese teams allow various companies to buy advertising space on the tickets. Among the biggest ticket advertisers are oil and automobile companies as well as sporting goods manufacturers.

Other worthwhile Japanese baseball collectibles include the annual record books published by the Central and Pacific leagues, individual team yearbooks and pennants.

The record books are styled along the lines of the annual U.S. *Official Baseball Guide* published for the major leagues by The Sporting News Co. of St. Louis, Mo. These annual record books can be easily used by the English-speaking baseball fan since the names of the players are given in English as well as in Kanji and statistics are statistics.

The yearbooks are as big and colorful as those published in the U.S.—there are team histories, player biographies, photos galore and loads of advertising.

Every team sells pennants at its souvenir stands with most of them changing the design of the pennant a little each year so that the fan will be induced to buy at least one every season. Featured vignettes in the pennants are the team logos.

Finally, many scores of postage stamps have been printed on the subject of baseball in Japan, stamps produced in Japan as well as in several other countries around the world. Postage stamps dealing with the diamond game are among the most interesting and least expensive of the baseball collectibles.

The Japanese Baseball Hall of Fame

In its own special building adjacent to Korakuen Stadium (now replaced by the Tokyo Dome), the Japanese Baseball Hall of Fame was dedicated in 1959. Election is not limited to players, but is open to anyone who played a significant part in the development of the game.

By 1990 the Hall of Fame at Tokyo had nearly 100 members. Represented there are those who organized and developed baseball in Japan during the last quarter of the 19th century; the most noted players and coaches from the country's colleges and universities; the organizers and builders of the professional leagues; and the great players and managers from the professional era.

Before a player from either the Central or Pacific Leagues can be considered for election, he must have been active on the field for at least five full years. (By contrast any American player must have been active for at least 10 seasons before he can be nominated for enshrinement in Cooperstown.)

The Baseball Hall of Fame in Tokyo pays proper tribute to

American major league stars as well. There are plaques of U.S. Hall of Famers as James "Pud" Galvin, Cy Young, Eddie Plank, Christy Mathewson, Grover Cleveland Alexander, John Clarkson, Tim Keefe, Walter Johnson, Lefty Grove, Rube Waddell and Warren Spahn. Their photos are also included in this special display.

In another part of the building, photos and brief career synopses of other great figures in U.S. baseball are included: Henry Chadwick, Judge Kenesaw Mountain Landis, John McGraw, Ty Cobb, Honus Wagner, Tris Speaker, Lou Gehrig, Babe Ruth, Joe DiMaggio, Ted Williams, Stan Musial, Mickey Mantle and others are represented.

DiMaggio played his final game in a Yankee uniform as a member of "Lefty O'Doul's All-Stars" who toured Japan in a fall 1951 exhibition series. On Dec. 11, less than two weeks after he arrived back in New York, DiMaggio announced his retirement from the game. DiMag was regarded as such a hero in Japan that he was invited to attend Emperor Hirohito's 50th wedding anniversary celebration in Jan. 1974.

Photos of every U.S. major league club that played an exhibition series in Japan are here, from the 1908 Reach All-Americans to the most recent team of touring Occidentals.

The Japanese Turn Professional

Inspired by the financial and artistic success of the 1934 American League Stars tour, a group of businessmen and sportsmen in Japan thought that it was about time for the country to form its own professional baseball league.

Even while the American League Stars were still in Japan, the Yomiuri Giants was organized by the Yomiuri newspaper owner, Matsutaro Shoriki. But it wasn't until 1936 that the professional league began actual competitive play. In the past, corporations had sponsored numerous baseball teams, but they were managed strictly on an amateur basis. The Yomiuri Giants, known also as Tokyo Giants—were given a "test run" in the summer of 1935, playing exhibition games against various corporation and college teams. At the same time, Shoriki, interested other businessmen in a new baseball circuit, the Japanese Professional Baseball League. (In 1950, when the Japanese Pacific League was formed, the Japanese Professional League changed its name to the Central League). Shoriki's efforts were almost entirely successful and seven teams, based in Tokyo, Osaka and Nagoya, were ready for competitive play the following year. In 1937, an eighth team was added.

In order to get his Tokyo Giants into shape in 1936, Shoriki sent his entire squad to California to take their spring training with Lefty O'Doul's San Francisco Seals. The March 1 encounter between the teams in San Francisco was particularly noteworthy. Eiji Sawamura, as crafty and brilliant as ever, pitched the Giants to a 5-0 victory over the Seals as he allowed only 3 hits and struck out 10.

The Tokyo Giants dominated baseball in Japan from the very beginning. No individual pennant winner was declared in 1936 since the 7 teams played in a series of tournaments, but from 1937 through 1944, the Giants won 6 pennants in those 8 seasons.

The 1944 season was cancelled after the first 35 games or so because of World War II, while the 1945 campaign was called off completely. Play, however, was resumed in 1946.

"A Real World Series"

Perhaps the Japanese are not yet ready to take on the Americans in what is supposed to be "A Real World Series"—that is, a series of games involving the winners of the U.S. World Series and the Japan Series. Nevertheless, this has for years been a topic of ongoing discussion in baseball circles everywhere in Japan.

Though the Japanese up to the present have not mounted a serious challenge for world parity or supremacy in baseball, it's still abundantly clear they've done extremely well in adopting an American game as their own, and nowhere in the world is baseball played with more uninhibited enthusiasm.

Index

Aaron, Hank, 96, 135
Adams, Maude, 30
Alexander, Charles, 141
Alexander, Grover, 141
Alexander, Grover Cleveland, 81, 98, 129, 156
Angell, Roger, 135
Allen, Johnny, 41
Allen, Woody, 107
American Card Catalog, 22, 30
Anson, Adrian C. (Cap), 24, 140
Appel, Marty, 108
Appling, Luke, 58, 140
Asinof, Eliot, 34, 136
Auctions, 81–88
Autographed Baseballs, 111–131
Averill, Earl, 41, 149, 150, 152–53

Bagby, Jim, 32, 34
Baker, Frank (Home Run), 81
Bancroft, Dave (Beauty), 4
Banks, Ernie, 113
Barlick, Al, 42
Barrett, Marty, 108
Baseball Cards, 12–48
Baseball Cards magazine, 48, 78, 133, 137, 138, 142
Baseball Cards News, 78, 133, 137
Baseball Stamps and Covers, 89–99
Baum, Fred, 21
Beckley, Jake, 24
Bench, Johnny, 140
Bennett, Charlie, 26
Berg, Moe, 149
Bishop, Max, 33
Boyer, Clete, 154
Boudreau, Lou, 97, 98
Bouton, Jim, 135
Boyd, Brendan C., 136–37
Bradley, Bill, 9, 122, 123
Bresnahan, Roger (Duke), 108
Brock, Lou, 59
Brosnan, Jim, 142
Brouthers, Dan, 24, 106
Brown, Clint, 149
Brown, Mordecai (Three-Finger), 28–29, 81
Browning, Pete, 24
Brush, John T., 70
Brush Rules, 70–71
Brown, Tom, 17
Bulkeley, Morgan G., 51
Burdick, Jefferson R., 15–16, 18, 21–24, 30, 31–32, 34
Burkett, Jesse (Crab), 24
Byrd, Sam, 85

Campanella, Roy, 92–93
Campbell, Bruce, 41

Canadian Sportscard Collector, 137
Cannon, Jimmy, 139
Card Collector's Bulletin, 18
Cards
   Allen & Ginter Cigarettes, 24, 26; American Caramels, 32; Baseball Legends (gum), 36, 44; Batter-up (gum), 41; Bowman Chewing Gum, 40; Buchner "Gold Coin Chewing Tobacco," 17; Cracker Jack (candy), 29, 81; Diamond Stars (National Chicle), 41, 134; Dog's Head Cigarettes, 20, 22; Donruss, 13; Fatima Cigarettes, 26; Fez Cigarettes, 28; Forst, Scott, personal baseball card, 75; Goudey Chewing Gum, 14, 38–39, 41; Hassan Cigarettes, 26; Japanese cards, 151, 153–54; Mecca Cigarettes, 26; Napoleon Cigarettes, 26; Obak cigarettes, 26; Old Judge Cigarettes, 18–20, 22, 24; Old Mill Cigarettes, 26, 28; Pacific Trading Cards ("Eight Men Out" series), 34–35, 147; Piedmont Cigarettes, 26; Play Ball (gum), 41; Ramly Turkish Cigarettes, 27; Score, 37; *Sporting Life* magazine, 25; "Strip" cards, 4; Sweet Caporal Cigarettes, 21, 26, 28, 31, 134; Topps Chewing Gum, 13, 33, 40, 46, 47, 95; "Turkey Reds" (cigarettes), 26, 30; Umpire cards, 42; Upper Deck, 47; Zeenuts (Candy), 33
Carlton, Steve, 94, 113–14, 122
Carrigan, Bill (Rough), 27
Cartwright, Alexander, 63–64
Caruthers, Bob, 24
Cascarella, Joe, 149
"Casey at the Bat," 143–45
Chandler, Albert Benjamin (Happy), 121–22
Chapman, Ben, 86
Chase, Hal, 28
Chesbro, Jack, 45
Chicago "Black Sox," 36
Cicotte, Eddie, 35
Clark, Peter, 66
Clark, Stephen Carlton, 55, 57–58, 65, 70
Clark, Will, 133
Clarkson, John, 20, 24, 156
Cleland, Alexander, 55
Clemente, Roberto, 93
Cobb, Jim, 101

Cobb, Ty, 14, 21, 28, 57, 67, 81, 90, 92–94, 98, 101, 130–31, 141, 156
Collins, Eddie, 28, 81, 98, 147
Combs, Earle, 85
Comiskey, Charles A. (Old Roman), 17, 22, 24, 70
Comiskey Park, 146–47
Conigliaro, Tony, 40
Connally, Tom, 42
Conlan, John Bertrand (Jocko), 42
Connor, Roger, 107–08
Cooper, James Fenimore, 41
Crawford, Sam, 28
Creamer, Robert W., 135
Critz, Hugh, 38–39
Cummings, William (Candy), 64

Daguerreotypes of Great Stars of Baseball, 26
Dahlen, Bill (Bad Bill), 28, 29
Dean, Jerome (Dizzy), 66
Deshong, Jimmy, 86
Dickey, Bill, 122
DiMaggio, Joe, 90, 92–94, 110, 112, 114–115, 120, 123, 156
Doby, Larry, 154
Dodger Stadium, 91, 141
Doerr, Bobby, 140
Donlin, Mike (Turkey Mike), 32
Doubleday Field, 55, 61, 145
Doubleday, General Abner, 51–55, 57, 63, 64
Dowd, John, 137
Dugan, Joe (Jumpin' Joe), 32, 86

Ebbets Field, Brooklyn, 99
Einstein, Charles, 141–42
Elberfeld, Norman (Tabasco Kid), 28
Elster, Kevin, 47
Elysian Fields, Hoboken, 55, 63–64
Erskine, Carl, 98–99
Evans, Billy, 42
Ewing, William (Buck), 24

Farley, James A., 59
Feller, Bob, 41, 127–29
Ferrell, Rick, 122
Fetzer, John E., 50, 61
Fetzer-Yawkey Building, Hall of Fame, 50, 60, 61, 63
Fischer, Rube, 87
Fitzsimmons, Fred, 38–39
Forbes Field, Pittsburgh, 66
Forst, Scott, 74–76, 98–99
Foxx, Jimmie, 139, 149, 150
Frick, Ford, 57–59, 61

Galvin, James (Pud), 140, 156
Gasparro, Frank, 67
Gehrig, Lou, 62, 81–83, 85, 92–93, 105–06, 149, 150, 153, 154, 156

Acknowledgments

Special thanks are due to Barry Halper who has assisted us liberally in a variety of writing projects. In particular, we're indebted to Barry, America's premier collector of baseball memorabilia, for supplying us with a wide array of photos. Special thanks also to Joseph H. Rose, president of Harmer Rooke Galleries, New York City, for supplying a number of vintage baseball card illustrations.

We must also acknowledge the efforts poured into this volume by David A. Boehm, editor-in-chief of Sterling Publishing Co., Inc. David is the perfect editor for a book of this type since he's followed the game of baseball closely for more than a half-century and has never lost his enthusiasm. Moreover, he usually sees things my way in regard to a book's editorial content and overall format if I present a convincing enough argument.